Tongues Of Fire

New Life
In The Spirit

John A. Stroman

CSS Publishing Company, Inc.
Lima, Ohio

TONGUES OF FIRE

Library of Congress Cataloging-in-Publication Data

Stroman, John A.,
    Tongues of Fire : 12 sermons on new life in the Holy Spirit / John A. Stroman.
        p.   cm.
    Includes bibliographical references.
    ISBN 0-7880-0349-6
    1. Holy Spirit — Sermons. 2. Christian life — Sermons. 3. Sermons, American.
I. Title.
BT121.2.S88   1995
231'.3—dc20   94-36867
                                                                        CIP

This book is available in the following formats, listed by ISBN:
0-7880-0349-6 Book

PRINTED IN U.S.A.

Dedicated to

All those wonderful and thoughtful people who share in my Bible study groups at Pasadena Community Church. Their support, prayers and comments have made this volume possible.

Table Of Contents

Introduction

I feel somewhat like J. B. Phillips, in the Preface to his book, *The Young Church In Action,* a translation of the Book of Acts. He said it is easy for us to "write off" this little history of the Church's first beginnings as simply an account of a rather enthusiastic, emotional, and illogical religious experience resulting from ill-regulated and unorganized adolescence. The church in Acts provides us with both hope and judgment. Hope in the sense of what the church could be and judgment in the sense of what we have failed to be.

What has followed from that New Testament experience of the Holy Spirit has been a well-disciplined maturity by the church through the ages in which the embarrassing earlier irregularities no longer appear. I am convinced that in this process we in the present church have lost something. The spontaneity of the Spirit has been replaced by the accommodations we have sought to make between the Christian life and middle class cultural values. When we compare the strength and vigor of the early church with the confused and sometimes feeble performance of the divided church today, we have to admit that the early Church was open "on the Godward side of life" that is unknown to us.

There are certain patterns that have come out of the experience of Pentecost in Acts 2. My purpose in this writing is to discover what those patterns are and what meaning they have for us today. These patterns of Pentecost, i.e., the language, scope, and the promise of Spirit are important aspects of our life in the Spirit. I have given serious thought to the charismatic renewal movement of our time which has captured a new sense of life in the Spirit. It has brought emotion, feeling and excitement to Christian experience. If you have ever attended a Pentecostal worship service you are amazed by the unaccustomed sight of seeing worshippers glad they are there, singing the hymns like they enjoy them, and all having a good

7

time. Leonard Sweet declared, "That not since the eighteenth-century Wesleyan revival has there been such a genuine stirring of the Spirit."

It is not a question of the Holy Spirit's activity in our midst, but our awareness of where that activity is taking place. The Holy Spirit is involved in the age-old struggle against every form of evil that threatens to enslave human life, while at the same time establishing communities of meaning, covenant, freedom and hope. How many times has the Holy Spirit been grieved by the refusal of Christians to support change in human life and direction? Nevertheless, the Holy Spirit still leads us toward the future. The two biblical symbols of the Holy spirit are wind and fire. These two symbols suggest a fierce ferociousness and tremendous power, but above all they are unpredictable. So is life in the Spirit. Jesus reminded us, "The wind blows where it wills, and you hear the sound of it, but you do not know whence it comes or whither it goes; so it is with every one who is born of the Spirit" (John 3:8).

Near the end of the book I have a chapter on the Trinity. I have dealt with it out of necessity. A book on new life in the Spirit must deal with the Trinity. Christian theology begins, continues, and ends with the inexhaustible mystery of God. The Trinity helps us to deal with this mystery and is basic to our understanding of Christian experience.

I am indebted to the congregation at Rader Memorial United Methodist Church in Miami who taught me how beautiful and alive a rainbow congregation of different races and cultures in the Holy Spirit could be. The members of my current parish, Pasadena Community Church in St. Petersburg, and especially those within my Bible study groups, have shared in much of this material and have responded with helpful and thoughtful feedback.

I want to thank my wife Vivian, whose careful reading of the text and continual support, has made all of this possible.

John A. Stroman
Pasadena Community Church
St. Petersburg, Florida

Chapter One

Who Is The Holy Spirit?

Why is there such renewed interest in the Holy Spirit? One answer is because there had been such widespread neglect of the Holy Spirit for so long. The emphasis on the Holy Spirit is one of the greatest developments in the past 20 years.

Through this period of charismatic renewal we have come to understand that when the church neglects the Holy Spirit religion deteriorates into a lifeless and dreary system of rules and ceremonies. It then becomes content with a "diminished mode of consciousness" and produces a condition of spiritual famine. The fact is, the doctrine of the Holy Spirit has never received the attention that other doctrines, such as Christology and the authority of Scripture have. There have been those moments in church history when the official church opposed movements that have stressed the presence and the power of the Spirit. This was evident in the second century when the church opposed the Montanists; in the twelfth century the Waldensians, in the sixteenth century the Anabaptists, and the charismatic and Christian base communities of our time.

Neglect and suspicion of the work of the Holy Spirit has had a damaging effect on both the Christian life and Christian theology. Daniel L. Migliore in his book, *Faith Seeking Understanding,* stresses the fact that such neglect "can lead to distortions in the understanding of God, the doctrine of Scripture, the significance of the natural order, the value of human culture, the interpretation of Christ and his work, the nature of the church, the freedom of the Christian, and hope for the final fulfillment of life" (p. 166).

Migliore is careful to point out that when the work of the Holy Spirit is suppressed, the power of God is then understood as distant, hierarchical, and coercive. The neglect of the Holy Spirit causes the church to be seen as a rigid power structure in which certain members rule over others, and the sacraments degenerate into almost magical rites under the control of a clerical elite.

However, it can no longer be said that the church in the United States has kept the Holy Spirit behind closed doors. In recent years we have witnessed a resurgence of interest in the Holy Spirit and Christian spirituality. The emphasis on the Holy Spirit has been one of the greatest religious developments in the past 20 years. But even with the rise and increase of the christmatic movement there continues to be little theological rigor or reflection. Experience and understanding are two different things.

A Renewed Interest In The Holy Spirit

The resurgence of interest in the Holy Spirit has been tied to the renewed interest in Christian spirituality. Therefore numerous factors have contributed to this renewed interest in the Spirit.

1) It is a reaction against the formal, depersonalized, bureaucratic life of the mainline churches. As Daniel Migliore points out it is a protest from the rank and file of the membership who are not happy about the domination of form over vitality, structure over purpose, and external authority over free consent.

2) Our technological society, which has been described as one of "high tech" and "low touch," has produced isolation and loneliness. There is a desire for new life, new community, and new joy that has created a new interest in a new spirituality in the Holy Spirit.

3) In the '60s and '70s countless pastors and lay people were involved in various social and political movements of reform. The spiritual life was neglected at the expense of social activism. It is now apparent that the struggles for justice, freedom, and peace can only be achieved through a life that is sustained by spiritual vitality. It is interesting that many liberation theologians have produced new works in the field of spiritual formations, i.e., biblical studies, worship and prayer. This hunger for a deeper faith has created a new interest in the Holy Spirit.

4) The development of the ecumenical church has placed a new interest in the Holy Spirit. Migliore has pointed out that there are three factors that have contributed to this: the phenomenal expansion of the Pentecostal and charismatic churches; the growing influence of the Eastern Orthodox Churches that have argued for centuries that the Western churches' theology of the Spirit is defective; and the emergence of the Christian base communities in Latin America and other places around the world.

5) It is suggested by Leonard Sweet that the charismatic renewal is a reaction against atrophied feelings at worship, against bolt-down pews, sit-down services and stone-faced monologues. Regardless of what one thinks about the neo-charismatic movement it is a force to be reckoned with and those involved have made religion exciting. They go to church and enjoy it. They sing the hymns with enthusiasm like they believe the words. The Bible is so important to them that they read it and study it. There is a sense of euphoria about their overall religious experience.

It is the contention of many Christian historians and theologians that after such a long period of concentration on Christology in Western theology, it is now time to shift direction to pneumatology (the study of the Holy Spirit).

With all of the renewed interest in the Holy Spirit, there is still in the charismatic movement a lack of theological rigor. Leonard Sweet said that the reason our understanding of the Spirit is shallow even when our experience may be deep hit home for him one day when a Doctor of Ministry student informed him that he never preached to his congregation on the doctrine of the Holy Spirit because they could not understand the Spirit. No wonder that so many Christian minds have not given any serious thought or reflection on the Holy Spirit or the

Trinity. No wonder we are so bereft of theological understanding of the nature and the function of the Holy Spirit. It would not be surprising to have church members respond to us as they did to the apostle Paul in Ephesus, "We have never heard that there is a Holy Spirit" (Acts 19:2).

Who Is The Holy Spirit?

Perhaps the best place to start is by asking the question, *Who is the Holy Spirit?* In answering this question it is evident that both individuals and denominations tend to emphasize one aspect of the Holy Spirit at the expense of another. The result is that we get a one-sided Christian or denominational division resulting in a misunderstanding of the Holy Spirit.

There are Christians who have an experience of the Spirit that emphasizes *vitality* and intensity of feeling and emotion. They have a tendency to be impatient and at times critical of those Christians whom they consider to be intellectual and cold as they emphasize doctrine and truth. They tend to be highly individualistic without appreciation for the "forms" and "structures" of the organized church. At times there is even antagonism toward other church members who do not share in these personal religious experiences.

Along this same line of vitality and emotion is the phenomenon of speaking in tongues. It should not be dismissed as being of no spiritual importance, nor should it be over-exaggerated. The charismatic movement has played a very positive role in recovering and re-emphasizing the centrality of experience in the spiritual life. At the same time one of the shortcomings of the movement has been its division of Christians into first-class and second-class citizens. I will deal with the gifts of the spirit and the charismatic Christian in a later chapter.

On the other hand there are those Christians who emphasize *authority*. They fight against heresy in their quest for "pure doctrine" and a "pure church," whatever that means. For them this is what really counts. Religion is a head trip, cerebral. The maintenance of orthodoxy is their primary concern. They have a tendency to be critical of the church at large, because it contains too many people who do not think and act as they do.

There are other people who see themselves as Spirit-filled Christians who emphasize *solidarity*. Their desire is to maintain the unity of the church at all cost. They have a deep appreciation for the community of the Holy Spirit. All of these other facets of church life are all right as long as they do not disturb the order and the stability of the church.

The result of all of this is that we have three gifts of the same Spirit and they have a tendency to lead to three conflicting ideas of the Christian life. The fact is that all three of these characteristics are genuine aspects of the Holy Spirit. Christianity is a heart-felt religion of emotion and feeling. Glossolalia, the speaking in tongues, is a gift of the Spirit. Christianity is a religion of authority and power. It is a religion of solidarity with a strong emphasis on community. Each of these are important aspects of the life of the Holy Spirit, but one should not be expressed at the expense of another. In chapter three we will look at one of the main functions of the Holy Spirit as being the Spirit's desire to maintain and establish community.

The fact remains that where the Holy Spirit is at work there is new life, enthusiasm, emotion and feeling, as well as, truth and community. A more careful study of the Holy Spirit would be helpful to us so as not to emphasize one aspect of the Spirit to the detriment of another. I agree with Shirley C. Guthrie's conclusion in regard to the Holy Spirit when he states that "many theologians today believe that, as the church concentrated on the person of Christ for centuries, we in our time, with our problems, need to give special attention to the Spirit."

The Holy Spirit Is A Person

The Holy Spirit is God, not a something but a Someone. John Macquarrie states that the Holy Spirit is God coming to men and women in an inward way to enlighten and to strengthen. Guthrie points out that we have a tendency to think of the Holy Spirit in an impersonal manner as a source of energy. He said a common but misleading analogy is to think of the Spirit being like electricity. If we get plugged into the Spirit then power will flow into our lives. This is a mistaken analogy because it is so impersonal. To depersonalize the Spirit is to depersonalize human beings. The Holy Spirit of God is not a kind of spiritual electric current, nor are human beings light bulbs to be turned on and off. But the Holy Spirit works personally, treating us not as objects to be manipulated, but as conscious, thinking, willing persons. (See Guthrie, *Christian Doctrine,* p. 293.)

The Holy Spirit Is Lord

If the Holy Spirit is the Spirit of God the Father and God the Son, then the Spirit too is the Lord. This is expressed by Paul in 2 Corinthians 3:17, "Now the Lord is the Spirit, and where the Spirit of the Lord is, there is freedom." Guthrie points out that the Holy Spirit is not the prisoner of the church, nor an exclusive possession of Christians. "The wind (Spirit) blows where it wills" (John 3:8). He is Lord. The Spirit works wherever and whenever the Spirit chooses. Although the Spirit works within the individual and the church, the Spirit is not limited to work only in the Christian community and the hearts of individual believers. We never own the Spirit in the sense that we can take ownership of the Spirit. "Whenever we see new life achieved, new truth discovered, new communities overcoming old divisions and hostility, there we may thankfully recognize the work of the Holy Spirit" (Guthrie, *ibid.,* p. 294).

Robert McAfee Brown points out that the church between Ascension and Pentecost is a picture of what the church must always be, a group of people gathered together praying for, waiting for, the coming of the Holy Spirit. The church does not "have" the spirit, nor does the church "possess" the

Spirit. The church can only wait for the Spirit and live in dependence upon the Spirit *(The Spirit Of Protestantism,* p. 49). In another chapter I will attempt further doctrinal comment as I deal with the Trinity.

The Holy Spirit And Conflict

Although the Holy Spirit is seeking to create community there are those anticommunity forces that are always at work. How can the Holy Spirit help to resolve the tensions between the forces that work to disrupt and those that seek to maintain community?

In every living organism there is conflict. Even within the church, as a dynamic living social organism, tension exists. Although conflict appears inevitable, the fear is that it may become divisive and weakening. However, for there to be life, there must be tension. The history of the Christian church is a long and ardent story of struggle and tension. This is true from the Council of Jerusalem in Acts 15, to the ecumenical councils at Nicea and at Chalcedon, to the Council of Trent, as well as the Second Vatican Council in our own time.

This is to say nothing about the debates and discussions on matters of faith and ethics that annually involve synods, presbyteries, and church conferences of various denominations across the land where tensions are high and conflict is unavoidable. The life of the church, if it is alive in the Spirit, is one of tension and conflict.

The Holy Spirit can cause chaos to be creative. The Holy Spirit is the integrative element within community. Integration is not a melting process; it does not result in a bland average. Rather I would think of it as a rainbow with a sense of beauty and wonder, while each color is distinct. The Holy Spirit fosters openness, while protecting uniqueness and individuality. The Christian community does not solve the problem of pluralism by obliterating diversity. The Spirit seeks out diversity, welcomes different points of view, embraces opposites and desires to see the other side of every issue. The Holy

Spirit is "wholistic." Above all, the Holy Spirit makes the community safe for diversity. In a sense the Spirit unifies as the Spirit diversifies. The Spirit promotes unity by preserving diversity, thus creating a community of growth and creativity.

Diversity — A Source Of Spiritual Power

Historically the Holy Spirit within the Christian community has sought an openness with a free exchange of ideas as a means of maintaining creativity. If the Christian community sought uniformity of method or thought then life together would be dull indeed, and creativity minimized. The Christians at Pentecost discovered that their diversity was an amazing source of spiritual power. Take a close look at the events surrounding Pentecost in Acts 2 and the development of the early Christian community within the biblical narrative and you discover that conflict is a given.

Today life in the church has not changed. It is still characterized by controversy. The conflict in Acts 15 was in regard to the many opinions over the need to follow Jewish laws and circumcision. It was a heated and deep-seated debate. Today the conflict continues but the issues have changed. The current issues are those regarding abortion, capital punishment, euthanasia, poverty, race, war and homosexuality. These current issues are so explosive and divisive it would seem impossible to ever suggest any possible unanimity within a denomination or a congregation.

It is rather presumptuous to think that the church could ever avoid such controversy, nor should it desire to do so. There are issues that must be faced. It is sad indeed to see congregations being built around single issues, but that is taking place. Regrettably, what unites some congregations is the dislike they have for the congregations they have left. Many congregations are built around a single theological position that permits just one approach to social issues.

The unity of some congregations is maintained by the strict adherence to a creedal statement or to the wholehearted

16

agreement with the pastor. People with opposing points of view, either with the creed or the preacher, are asked to leave. Fundamental Southern Baptist seminary leaders have issued an ultimatum to their seminary professors who deviate ever so slightly from their fundamentalist point of view: "resign or be dealt with harshly." It would seem to me that to force the moderates out of the Southern Baptist Convention in such a manner would weaken the convention. Also, Cardinal John O'Connor of New York publicly warned Roman Catholic politicians who take a "pro-choice" stand on abortion that they "are at risk of excommunication." To muzzle dissent seems to betray the possible creativity in the Holy Spirit that the church experienced in Acts 2.

The Holy Spirit And The Christian Life

What is the relationship between the Holy Spirit and the Christian? The New Testament presents a multidimensional description of the work of the Holy Spirit. One of these dimensions is that the Holy Spirit presents Christ to the believers. Through the Holy Spirit Christ is a living presence among us. This is essentially the meaning of the Ascension in Acts 1. The Ascension was necessary. For just as in a moment of time Jesus entered the world, in a moment of time Jesus left the world. When Jesus left the world the period of resurrection had ended. This was the promise of Jesus in John 16:7, "Nevertheless, I tell you the truth: it is to your advantage that I go away, for if I do not go away, the Advocate will not come to you; but if I go, I will send him to you" (NRSV). The spatial limitations for Jesus are removed. Through the coming of the Holy Spirit Jesus was never more present than when he was absent.

Therefore, the Ascension brings an end to the story of Christ and ushers in the age of the Spirit. The Ascension is introductory to the account of Pentecost. The Ascension is the end of the old with Pentecost and the coming of the Holy Spirit as the beginning of the new. The first aspect of the Holy

Spirit is to make Christ present for all believers. The Spirit unites believers to Christ and thus spans the gap between the then and there and the here and now. Christ is not merely the memory of someone who has loved in the past, but he is a living presence here and now in the power of the Holy Spirit.

A second aspect of the Holy Spirit is the creation of a new life. In John 3, the Spirit is the agent of the Christian's new birth. Just as we were born from our mother's womb in our natural birth, we are born anew (again) by the Holy Spirit. Throughout the Book of Acts there is the emphasis on the Holy Spirit as the power of transformation from the old to the new, from the enslavement of sin and death to new life in the Spirit.

A third aspect of the work of the Holy Spirit is freedom. Paul writes in 2 Corinthians 3:17, "Where the Spirit of the Lord is, there is freedom." Throughout the scriptures there is the theme that the Spirit sets the prisoner free (Isaiah 42:1ff, 61:1ff). We must not overlook the fact that in the New Testament the work of Christ is essentially one of liberation and freedom, "For freedom Christ has set us free" (Galatians 5:1). The activity of the Holy Spirit is a continuation of the work begun in Christ.

Fourth, one of the most important aspects of the Holy Spirit is the desire for community. In the midst of our diversity it is the Holy Spirit that seeks to bring us together and unites us. It has been pointed out by Daniel Migliore that the unitive power of the Spirit is not mere togetherness of the like-minded or the kinship of people of the same family, race, economic class, or nation. It is a power of new community that unites strangers and even former enemies. The Holy Spirit creates community where formerly there were insuperable barriers. "There is no longer Jew or Greek, there is no longer slave or free, there is no longer male and female; for all of you are one in Christ Jesus" (Galatians 3:28 NRSV). In Christ and by the power of the Holy Spirit we are one community. I will have more to say on the Holy Spirit and community in a later chapter.

18

A fifth aspect of the Holy Spirit is the ecstatic and illogical. At Pentecost the apostles were overwhelmed by the *charismata*. The charismata refers to the gifts of God's grace freely given through the Holy Spirit enabling the Christian to perform his or her service in the church, as well as defining a special gift enabling the Christian to perform a particular ministry in the church. Charismata is the plural form of charisma which refers to a special gift of God's grace. It was an emotional and enthusiastic experience, at times ecstatic and illogical.

In our celebration of Pentecost we need to ask the question, "What role did the non-rational and ecstatic play in Christian beginnings — and what role does it play in experiencing Christian life, being, and worship today?" During my seminary years we were trained not to trust our feelings or emotions. I am still somewhat of a rationalist seeking to express Christian experience, worship and social outreach in words that are sometimes oblivious to the fact that I am doing exactly that — reducing it all to a form of words and reason. I have come to realize that too much rationality can be as dangerous as too much non-rationality. I remember reading Bishop Butler's words to John Wesley, "Sir, the pretending to extraordinary revelations and gifts of the Holy Ghost is a horrid thing, a very horrid thing." James Dunn points out that Pentecost itself has all the marks of an ecstatic experience involving visions, audition and glossolalia.

It is easy for us today to write off this brief history of the church's inception at Pentecost as simply an account of enthusiastic but ill-regulated and unorganized adolescence of an infant church. With our current well-disciplined maturity we have been careful not to allow these embarrassing irregularities to appear among us in our mainline congregations. Yet when we compare the strength and vigor of the spirit-filled church at Pentecost with the confused and sometimes feeble performance of the divided body of Christ today I am convinced as J. B. Phillips said, "There is someone at work there besides merely human beings."

The Female Imagery Of The Spirit

What about the appropriateness of the female imagery of the Holy Spirit? It should be noted that the word for Spirit is feminine in Hebrew, *ruach,* although it is neuter in Greek, *pneuma*, and masculine in Latin, *spiritus.* The activities of the Spirit in the New Testament are those of nurturing. In the conversation with Nicodemus found in John 3, Jesus speaks of the work of the Spirit as like that of a mother. Some theologians suggest that the Holy Spirit is the feminine counterpart of the incarnate Son of God. (See Sally McFague's *Metaphorical Theology.)* It is suggested that a theology of the maternity of the Spirit could have a counterbalance to the excessive masculinity of the church's traditional imaging of God and its understanding of power. Daniel Migliore gives this cautious response by stating that God is beyond gender and that we must avoid the danger of making idols of our images and metaphors about God. "The triune God is neither an exclusive fraternity nor a divine company composed of two males and one female." That the triune God is also called Spirit teaches us to think and speak of God as uniquely personal, allowing gender-specific imagery, yet far transcending all such imagery. God is Spirit "and lives in perfect love and mutual interrelationships" (Migliore, *op.cit.* p. 174). There are many voices in contemporary theology suggesting that the loss of the feminine dimension in God has been a serious impoverishment and distortion of the Christian faith. There is much more to be said in this regard, because feminist theology is part of the emerging liberation movement.

For Further Reflection And Study

1. In what way has the neglect and suspicion of the work of the Holy Spirit had a damaging effect on both the Christian life and Christian church?

2. Why is there such renewed interest in the Holy Spirit?

3. Define the Holy Spirit in light of your personal experience and the Bible.

4. What difference does the Holy Spirit make in your life?

5. Which descriptions of the Holy Spirit: *vitality, authority,* or *solidarity* best characterize your understanding of the Holy Spirit? Explain.

6. How can conflict be creative within the Christian community?

7. What are your opinions regarding the ''female imagery'' of the Holy Spirit?

Chapter Two

Pentecost — A Wild, Weird, Wonderful Day

The happenings on the day of Pentecost seemed so bizarre with the sound of a rushing mighty wind, tongues of fire resting on the participants, and the speaking in other languages, that it caused the onlookers to conclude, "They are filled with new wine." In other words, "They are drunk!" Peter observed that they were confusing inspiration with inebriation so he declared, "Men of Judea and all who dwell in Jerusalem, let this be known to you, and give ear to my words. For these men are not drunk, as you suppose, since it is only the third hour of the day; but this is what was spoken by the prophet Joel" (Acts 2:14b-16).

A New Kind Of Power

Our world is a world of power. Political power. Military power. Financial power. Institutional power. A power that can be destructive to the human spirit and freedom, becoming restrictive, oppressive, confining, and threatening.

At Pentecost we celebrate the coming of a new kind of power. A power to set free. A power that can make the lame to walk, the blind to see, and release the addict from his addiction. A power to release the captive, that can turn boredom into usefulness, dreariness to radiance, and narcissistic self-centeredness to a life of joyous self-giving. I am talking about power that can take our dry bones of inactivity and listlessness and create a life of effervescent joy and radiance.

That power is the presence of the Holy Spirit. Jesus said to his disciples, "But you shall receive power when the Holy

Spirit has come upon you ....'' On that first Pentecost, 120 lukewarm believers were ignited with the flame and zeal of the Holy Spirit. On that day Peter stood up and preached the sermon of his life and before the day ended over 3,000 people committed themselves to the Christian way. These courageous and committed souls went out and in the words of Luke "turned the world upside down." This is why we call Pentecost the birthday of the church. It is a wild, weird and wonderful day that burst upon Jerusalem nearly 2,000 years ago.

Expansion And Growth

This experience was highly contagious. It spread rapidly from Jerusalem, to Judea, Samaria and to the ends of the earth. As we read the account of Pentecost we cannot help feeling disturbed. J.B. Phillips in his Introduction to his book, *The Young Church in Action,* points out that this is the way the church was meant to be. It was a vigorous and flexible church. How far removed we are from the experience of Pentecost. We have become fat and short of breath through prosperity, musclebound by over-organization, powerless because of our accommodation with culture, idolatrous because of our subservience to national and political values, and generic as an institution because of our capitulation to a civil religion. We might say that this church at Pentecost was uncomplicated and naive by modern standards, but we must admit they were open on the God-ward side in a way that is almost unknown to us today.

Look at the vitality of Pentecost. The greatest period of growth, expansion and moral influence of the Christian Church took place between Pentecost and the time of Constantine's Edict of Toleration in 311 A.D. that brought about the demise of the church resulting from the church's union with the Roman state and culture.

The Holy Spirit And Change

What a dramatic change came about at Pentecost, especially to the apostle Peter. We all remember what a vacillating person he was, so impetuous, outspoken and at times cowardly. Now he delivers one of the most magnificent sermons in the New Testament with unbelievable results. The remarkable change in Peter is evident the next day when he and John were going up to the temple to pray. At the gate of the temple was a lame man who asked them for alms. Peter said to him, "I have no silver and gold, but I give you what I have; in the name of Jesus Christ of Nazareth, walk" (Acts 3:6). Peter took him by the hand and raised him up, and leaping up, the man stood and walked. Do you see what the Holy Spirit did for Peter? Peter's life was like an ordinary piece of wire, that became incandescent with the Holy Spirit. If we would take a stethoscope and place it against the heart of the early church we would hear the throbbing life beat of the Holy Spirit.

As we consider the possibilities of new life in the Spirit, how can we define the nature of the Holy Spirit's power in our lives? Let me share with you three symbols that help clarify the kind of power the Holy Spirit brings.

The Wind Of The Spirit

First, the power of the Holy Spirit is like the *wind,* gentle yet forceful. The biblical words for "Spirit" are *ruach* in Hebrew and in Greek, *pneuma,* which are translated as breath, air or wind. Each suggests air that is in constant motion. The coming of the Holy Spirit was like "the rush of a mighty wind." Wind has unpredictable and certain dynamic qualities. There is the gentle breeze blowing off the gulf which is cool and refreshing. But those of us who live on the gulf coast of Florida also know of another wind, the ferocious, devastating wind of a hurricane, which at times can exceed 100 mph, toppling trees and leveling homes. That is the way it is with the Holy Spirit, gentle yet forceful.

The wind of the Spirit in the Bible is seen as the *breath of God.* It is God's instrument in overcoming chaos. In Genesis 1 it is the Spirit that moves over the face of the deep, bringing order out of darkness and confusion. Again when God breathed into a lump of clay man became a living soul. The wind of the Spirit is life-giving.

We see this in Ezekiel 37. Here the Lord sat Ezekiel down in the valley of dry bones and said to him, "Ezekiel, can these dry bones live?" Ezekiel said, "O dry bones, hear the word of the Lord." Look what happened: The wind of the Spirit entered them and they had life. If that can happen for Ezekiel in the valley of dry bones, think what can happen when the Holy Spirit, the breath of God, breathes upon us and these dry bones of ours? When the breath of God breathes over the smoldering coals of our lives, latent with potential, they come aglow. It is much like what happens when we are barbecuing in the backyard and we blow our breath over the smoldering coals causing them to glow and burst into flames. The breath of the Holy Spirit causes our life to burst with new flames of life and vitality.

We need to catch the wind of the Spirit in our sails and it will carry us to new places and discoveries. When we were in Miami friends invited us to go with them to the Columbus Day Regatta on Biscayne Bay. They took us in their boat to the place where the sailboats turned around. As soon as the boats made their turn running before the wind they let out their spinnakers, which are large triangular sails in the most brilliant and spectacular colors. It was a marvelous sight with the blue sky, aqua water of the bay and the sparkling colors of the sails. It was glorious. That's what it's like to have the Holy Spirit in your life: to run before the wind with your spinnaker full.

The Oil Of The Spirit

Second, the power of the Holy Spirit is like *oil,* soothing, comforting and healing. Oil in the Bible has been associated with anointing. A person who was called of God was anointed with oil, set apart for special responsibilities. The anointing was a time of preparation and readiness for the service of God. Moses poured oil over Aaron's head, beard, and robe consecrating him for service. Samuel anointed David with oil, authenticating his selection by God as one who was to perform great duties. Elijah anointed kings and prophets with oil, setting them apart for special responsibilities. When Jesus began his public ministry, for his inaugural address he chose the anointing passage from Isaiah 61:1, by beginning his sermon, "The Spirit of the Lord is upon me because he has *anointed* me to bring good tidings to the afflicted ...."

From the day of Pentecost the oil of God's Spirit continues to flow upon all Christians sanctifying them for service. This has particular meaning for you and me. This is not something that happens at one time, but there is the fresh anointing of God's Spirit for every new task that we face. God anoints us with the Spirit in preparation for whatever life brings our way, preparing us to face anything. How many times have you survived a situation or an experience that you thought you could never endure? As you look back upon it you realize that it was the presence of God's Spirit in your life that brought you through. You reached the breaking point but you did not break. You came to the end of your rope, but miraculously there was more rope. You came to the end of your strength, but you had renewed strength, because there was a fresh anointing of the Holy Spirit for that new task.

Oil is also symbolic of the healing power of the Holy Spirit. The Holy Spirit brings a healing power into our lives and into our life together as the body of Christ. It has been the practice of the church for centuries to anoint a person with oil along with the laying on of hands to bring about healing. The oil used in the Bible for anointing was olive oil. The olive branch traditionally has been a symbol of healing and peace.

We need this healing presence of the Holy Spirit in our personal lives, because we are a wounded people in need of healing. Also we need the healing presence of the Holy Spirit in our church community. Our only hope for unity and togetherness amid our diversity is the presence of the Spirit. Left to ourselves we are a divided and fragmented people. Although we may speak with many accents because we are a people of various races and cultures, yet because of the Spirit's presence we speak one language — the language of love. The Spirit makes it possible for us to overcome the barriers and obstacles that seek to divide us.

The oil in your automobile engine makes it possible for all the parts to work together. It lessens friction and heat and keeps the engine from wearing out. That's the nature of the Holy Spirit's work within your life: to lessen friction and heat and to keep you from wearing out. A life without the Holy Spirit is one of friction and confrontation, making it more difficult to get along with others. The Spirit's presence in our lives is one of joy, sweetness, excitement and praise. Did you know that Jonathan Edwards, that nineteenth century preacher known for his sermon, "Sinners in the Hands of an Angry God," had as his favorite word "sweet"? God is above all a God of sweetness, enthusiasm, joy, and openness. God's mortal enemies are complacency, sourness, mediocrity, discouragement and boredom. Jesus may have been a man of sorrows acquainted with grief, but he was also a man of laughter acquainted with joy. When the Holy Spirit is present in a heterogeneous and diverse congregation we can sing, "There is a sweet, sweet spirit in this place and I know it's the Spirit of the Lord."

The Fire Of The Spirit

Third, the power of the Holy Spirit is like *fire*, all-consuming and purifying. Fire is the most alluring and most menacing of all the symbols of the Holy Spirit. John the Baptist said, "I baptize you with water . . . he (Jesus) will baptize you with the Holy Spirit and fire."

Fire in the scriptures is a symbol of God's presence, a description of theophany throughout the biblical narrative. This is evident in Abraham's covenant experience; the burning bush with Moses; Yahweh's leading Israel by the pillar of fire by night and Yahweh's appearance in fire on Mt. Sinai.

The ever-burning fire on the altar of Leviticus 6:12 reveals the continual presence of God. In the experience of biblical history, fire is seen as purification, particularly in the Babylonian exile (Isaiah 43:2). The reference in the New Testament to the baptism by fire surely contains the idea of refining and purification. Fire, as a metaphor of God's holiness mediated through the Holy Spirit, may destroy or purge, but the Spirit does not leave men and women comfortably alone.

The Holy Spirit as fire suggests enthusiasm. If we as church members do not get excited about our church, we are not going to excite anyone else. If we are not enthusiastic, we are not going to enthuse others. John Killinger in his book, *For God's Sake, Be Human,* tells about a wife who came into her husband's bedroom on Sunday morning, threw open the curtains and pleaded with her husband to get out of bed. She said, "It is Sunday. Get up and get dressed; you'll be late for church." He replied, "I don't want to go to church. The choir sings off-key. The people are unfriendly, unresponsive and cold." She said, "You've got to get up and get going; you're the preacher." Pessimism can be just as contagious as enthusiasm. But a warm, spirit-filled life of joy and excitement can help other people to catch the same spirit.

The fire of enthusiasm and excitement attracts attention. The story is told about a church that caught fire long before they ever had fire trucks or hydrants. A bucket brigade was organized from the creek to the church. The preacher was rushing back and forth giving orders and he happened to notice at the head of the line was a man he had invited to church often, but who never came. He said to him, "John, this is the first time you have ever been to church." The man was quick to reply, "This is the first time the church ever caught on fire." Fire creates its own attraction.

The Miracle Of Pentecost

There were many things that took place at Pentecost. There was the strange speaking in tongues, the rush of a mighty wind, and the spectacle of tongues as of fire. The miracle of Pentecost was that they were able to hear and understand each other. This is why Paul lists the gifts of the Spirit, as healing, prophecy, teaching, tongues, and the "greatest" gift — love. Love brings an openness to one another. Love makes understanding possible.

Pentecost is the miracle of hearing being restored. Here were people from the four corners of the earth, different in language and culture, but they were able to hear one another. What a miracle. A miracle almost unknown in our world today.

> *Amazed and astonished, they asked, "Are not all of these speaking Galileans? And how is it that we hear, each of us in our own native language?"* — Acts 2:7-8 NRSV

It is the tragic inability to hear one another, to understand one another, that is miraculously healed at Pentecost. This is why Pentecost has been characterized as the Tower of Babel in reverse. Although the plan of God was frustrated in Genesis 11 it was accomplished in Acts 2. From Babel to Pentecost has been characterized as the movement from dissidence to harmony.

How tragic is this problem of our not being able to hear one another. Whites do not hear blacks. The affluent, you and I, do not hear the voices of the poor. Adults do not hear the muffled cries of the abused child. We have insulated ourselves from the agonizing voice of the AIDS victim. We seem to have given up on the power of Pentecost, which enables strangers to hear one another.

Many people in Jerusalem on the day of Pentecost were perplexed. "What does all of this mean?" they asked. "They are drunk on new wine," others mockingly replied. They were drunk, but not with new wine. They were drunk in what Edmund Steimle called "the dazzling possibilities of the love of God breaking out all over the place, smashing down barriers and opening our ears to one another."

The miracle of Pentecost assures us that the creative work of the Holy Spirit still seeks to restore us to what we were created to be, creatures able to hear and to understand each other.

For Further Reflection And Study

1. What were the distinguishing characteristics of the day of Pentecost?

2. Why do the happenings of Pentecost seem so strange to us today?

3. Describe the significance of fire, wind, and oil as symbols of the Holy Spirit. How do you relate the symbols to your personal understanding of the Spirit in your life?

4. Is it accurate to define Pentecost as the "birthday of the church"?

5. What aspects of Pentecost in Acts 2 are essential for the church today?

6. What is the significance of the Ascension of Jesus in Acts 1? What does it mean to say "that Jesus has never been as present to us as he is in his absence"?

Chapter Three

The Holy Spirit Creates Community

If the main function of the Holy Spirit is to create community, what kind of community does the Spirit seek to create? A community in the Holy Spirit is defined by Luke in Acts 2:43-47. Here Luke defines this community as one where:

- They devoted themselves to the apostle's teaching and fellowship.
- All who believed were together and had all things in common.
- They distributed what they had to each other, as any had need.
- They broke bread together in their homes.
- They spent much time in the temple (meaning in prayer and worship).
- They ate their food with glad and generous hearts.
- They praised God and had the goodwill of the people.
- Day by day the Lord added to their number those who were being saved.

This is the blueprint for a community of God's people. If you wonder where your church should be and what it should be about, here is the place to look. Here is the yardstick for measuring success.

In Acts we find a community created by the Holy Spirit that is a community not of creed, ministry or liturgy. These things were to come later. It was primarily a community that *stressed the immediacy of experience.* James D.G. Dunn has pointed out that there has always been one stream or strain of Christianity which has tended to play down the centrality of the written creed, of a properly ordered ministry of structure and worship, stressing rather the immediacy of experience.

John Wesley's experience of his "heart being strangely warmed" caused an emphasis to be placed on the personal experience of the Holy Spirit in early Methodism. Wesley placed importance on assurance. He declared, "The testimony of the Spirit is an inward impression on the soul, whereby the Spirit of God directly witnesses to my spirit that I am a child of God."

In the last half of the twentieth century the charismatic movement has gained an increasing recognition within the ecumenical church. If we are to ask, "Where is the church today?" we must also ask, "Where is the Holy Spirit recognizably present with power?" Two current examples that reflect this emphasis on experience and growth would be Africa and South Korea. However, it would be a mistake to describe these experiences of the Spirit in purely personal terms and lose sight of its corporate and communal aspects.

Luke's account of the early church reveals that religious experience shaped the church's character and formed its self-understanding in the first century. This gave rise to diverse manifestations, especially at the church at Corinth, but this diversity was a source of spiritual power. This is a lesson that we have not been able to learn. For the church today, diversity of religious thought and experience leads to conflict and chaos. There is no doubt that the church as it is described by Luke is unified by experience which manifests itself in a broad communal expression.

For Luke the Spirit is most clearly seen in extraordinary and obviously supernatural phenomena. The Spirit is the power that comes with a sound like a mighty wind and in visible tongues like fire (2:3); this power is clearly manifested in glossolalia (2:4, 10:46, 19:6). James Dunn points out that it is a power that affects its recipients in such a manner as to excite the wonder and the envy of an accomplished magician (8:18f). That is to say, when the power of the Spirit takes hold of someone in Luke's narrative, it manifests itself in an ecstatic experience. This is why Luke uses such dramatic language to describe the coming of the Spirit — "baptized into" (1:5), "came upon" (1:8), "poured out" (2:17ff), "fell upon" (8:16). This is why the question can be asked in 19:2, "Did you receive the Spirit when you became believers?" Because Luke's understanding of the Spirit is that of the enthusiast. Luke is one of those believers for whom spiritual experience must be visible, tangible, before it is able to serve as proof to others. What seemed to impress Luke most about earliest Christianity was its enthusiastic features.

Community Is Essential

Jurgen Moltmann points out in his book, *Creating a Just Future,* that we can only develop our personalities in regard to community. He goes on to say that the alternative to poverty is not property, but community. It is in the strength of community that we develop friendships. We find ultimate value and fulfillment in neighbors, colleagues, brothers and sisters, on whom we can rely in emergencies. Together, in community, we find solidarity, becoming strong enough to determine and shape our destinies. Therefore, the community is the true protector of personal freedom.

The only way men and women can live out "the image of God" is within community. Moltmann points out that the likeness of God cannot be lived out in isolation. It can only be lived out in human community. This means from the very beginning men and women who have been created in the "image of God" were social beings. Humans were created as gregarious beings and can only develop their personalities in fellowship with other people. "Isolated individuals are a deficient mode of human being, because they fall short of the likeness of God" (Moltmann, *ibid.,* p. 222f).

Within the biblical narrative, the Holy Spirit is the creator of community. What takes away from community is not of the Spirit. Hendrikus Berkhof, in his book *The Doctrine of the Holy Spirit,* points out that the chrismata may be interpreted as personal gifts, but they are not intended for private use. Spiritual gifts cannot be separated from the community of faith. The apostle states in 1 Corinthians 12:7 that the love gifts of the spirit are given for the enjoyment, employment and the edification of the community. They are given for the service of others, building up the church, and the communion of saints. We have a tendency to misunderstand the gifts of the Spirit because of the "individualism" that saturates American culture.

The Need For Community

Berkhof declares that "through community lies the salvation of the world." At this moment, nothing is more important. What characterizes the modern world more than anything else is our interrelatedness of the worldwide global community. Our survival as a human race depends on the success of community. Rugged individualism may have made this country in its early years, but our survival as a country now depends on our success of becoming a responsible member of the global community. This is a hard lesson for us to learn as American citizens as well as church members. We are suspicious of political international relationships and within our churches we have similar suspicions about ecumenical relationships within a global community of faith.

A person who is unrelated to community is a broken, alienated person. Leonard Sweet tells an Oriental story that illustrates this point.

> *A man crying from the depths of hell is pleading for release. When asked the good he has done in his life, all he can remember is that, while walking in the woods one day, he saw a spider and did not kill it. At once a silvery thread of a spider web is let down to him in hell. Grasping eagerly at this rope of hope, he is slowly lifted out of his misery. His fellow sufferers, seeing him about to escape, clutch his garment and his feet. Amazingly, all begin to be lifted up together. But the man, fearing the*

web might break, starts kicking at them, crying, "Let go!
Let go!" When they do let go, the thread breaks, and
all fall back into hell. The thread was strong enough for
a community of sufferers, but could not bear the heavy
burden of a selfish soul.

The Holy Spirit Creates Community

First, the Holy Spirit is the creator of community, because
new life produces a new community. To whom was the Holy
Spirit given on the Day of Pentecost? The Spirit was given to
a fellowship, to a community that was waiting for the Spirit's
coming. This community was following Jesus' instructions that
they prayerfully wait for the coming of the Spirit who would
bring to them power and teach them all things. What the Holy
Spirit created that day was not a creed, or a book, nor a theology, but a dynamic community known in the New Testament as "the Way." C. Norman Kraus stated this clearly in
his *The Community of the Spirit,* when he said, "To be saved
means to be in authentic relationship with fellow humans under the lordship of Christ. Salvation means the restoration of
community which the Old Testament prophets referred to as
the 'peace of God,' and which Jesus referred to as the kingdom of God."

The key purpose of Pentecost was the gift of community.
The experience of individual salvation is a most intense personal experience while at the same time it is a profoundly and
thoroughly social experience. Leonard Sweet's comment that
"any religion that ends with the self is finished" is accurate
(*New Life in the Spirit,* p. 68).

Making Community Safe For Diversity

Second, community in the Holy Spirit is "creative chaos."
Take a good look at the community of the Spirit and what
do you find? In Acts 2 it was a community of diversity: different nations, races and cultures. Those who were onlookers

37

said that they acted like a group of drunken men and women. To them it appeared like a chaotic situation. But Peter said to them, "These men are not drunk, as you suppose" (Acts 2:15). This was a creative chaos. There is unity but not at the expense of eliminating diversity.

The presence of the Holy Spirit comes among us to create community, not to destroy our differences. Unity in community is not achieved at the expense of diversity. The Holy Spirit respects our individuality. Certainly the Spirit is not interested in having those in community to think, act or speak the same. Unity in the Spirit does not mean uniformity. Within the Christian community "there are varieties of gifts, but the same Spirit; and varieties of services, but the same Lord; and there are varieties of activities, but it is the same God who activates all of them in everyone" (1 Corinthians 12:4-6 NRSV). The Spirit makes our community safe for diversity.

Unity Amid Diversity

Let me share with you an experience I had at Rader Memorial United Methodist Church in Miami. As pastor and people we were concerned to see if a rainbow assortment of people from different cultures, races and backgrounds could stay aglow within the same church family. Our desire was to maintain our diversity. We viewed our diversity as a plus, an attraction to newcomers and a source of creative interaction. Our rainbow congregation consisted of people from Puerto Rico, Belize, Granada, Jamaica, Haiti, the Dominican Republic, the Caribbean Islands, Nigeria, Sierra Leone, and the United States, both black and white.

Sunday morning worship served as the center in our quest for unity. We were a diverse people that Christ had called together. It was the centrifugal forces of our different cultures and traditions which sought to pull us apart. But the living presence of Christ, as the center of our community, was the centripetal force that pulled us together. Every Sunday in worship we affirmed the fact that we were a different people coming together to celebrate our oneness in Jesus Christ as Lord.

38

The celebration of the Eucharist every Sunday morning was the source of our unity and togetherness. As Protestants we have depended on verbal communication in worship. By setting this limit much is lost. But in the celebration of the Eucharist we discovered nonverbal communication in a dramatic form that cut across cultural, racial, and language barriers. By taking the bread and cup we communicated whereas before we were limited by our use of words. Although we had difficulty in understanding one another because of a language barrier, yet by holding and sharing together the sacrament we were able to communicate God's love in Jesus Christ.

Maintaining Diversity

We were a congregation diverse in culture and race. But Holy Spirit made it possible for us to maintain the rainbow, the protecting of each distinct color. In our worship there was diversity allowing for each cultural idiom to find meaning and expression. What appeared as chaotic was in fact creative. These moments of worship were joyous and celebrative bringing together the colorful diversity and beauty of the rainbow at the table of the Lord as we sang together, "We are one in the Spirit, we are one in the Lord." Maybe only then, but at least then.

The National Council of Churches gathered together representatives from 15 denominations in the United States and Canada to discuss the reason for the loss of young adults from the ages of 19 to 35 in their denominations. I thought Tex Sample, a professor at United Methodist-related St. Paul School of Theology in Kansas City provided some keen insight. He said that young adults will have political power when we have a mosaic society of ethnic diversity. He felt that the affluent members of today's churches attend primarily white or single-culture churches. These churches contrast strongly with the cultural and ethnic diversity of the world in which young adults live and work. Sample said we need a reprise of Pentecost to bridge our differences. He pointed out that in ten years, ethnic minorities are expected to account for nearly one-third of the U.S. population. And the people who are ethnic are the people who are young *(The United Methodist Reporter*, July 6, 1990). The Holy Spirit can bring together such diversity within our church.

The Holy Spirit As Integrative Element

Chaos is an unavoidable characteristic of the Christian community. There is always the chance that chaos would be divisive. The Holy Spirit is the integrative element in community, but integration is not a melting process. Consider our church board meetings. This is where we struggle with new ideas and strategy for ministry. This is where we share new concepts and new ways of doing things. This is where the old dies and the new seeks to be born and that is always a painful situation. The very presence of the Holy Spirit, whose character is vitality, liveliness, energy, venturesomeness, and fervor brings about the conflict of ideas and methods. It is the Spirit who leads us into new things. What appears as chaos to some is really new life in the Spirit who makes possible a creative chaos.

A man who had been married for 25 years told me he had never had a quarrel with his wife. Can you imagine that? I can't. Why is it that no quarrel or disagreement ever took place? Somebody in that relationship always gave in to the other person for 25 years. One partner in that relationship dominated the other, who remained silent out of fear. Would you call that a peaceful marriage? It is one of coercion more than peace. That is what can happen to a church board meeting. It can be quiet and peaceful when in fact it is dominated by a few and others are fearful to speak. Peace and quiet are not necessarily evidence of the Holy Spirit, but rather coercion where a group of board members may be afraid to speak their mind.

When I was in seminary I had a three-point charge. On Sunday morning I traveled to my first church for the 9 a.m. service, then I jumped into my car and traveled to my next service at 10 a.m., and then to my final service at 11 a.m. Even though it kept me on my toes they were joyous days. In the town where the parsonage was located there was a man who ran the only store in town. He ran the post office. As long as anyone could remember he was a member of the board of trustees and he ran the board. He was a member of the official board and people in the church referred to it as his board and his church. Those board meetings were quiet and peaceful, because he set the agenda and determined the vote on every item. There was no creative chaos in those board meetings. Because of his skillful planning the Holy Spirit did not have a ghost of a chance. Those board meetings never went beyond the level of his vision and insight.

Where the Holy Spirit creates community there is a free exchange of ideas, openness, and the opportunity for the honest expression of feelings. A member of our Administrative Board said to me recently, "I have just attended the best board meeting ever." I asked him why he felt that way. "Because I had a chance to speak," was his reply. See how much openness creates community. He now feels that he belongs and this is his church. Conflict that is genuine, creative, and peaceful is a sign of life and vigor. The Holy Spirit creates a creative chaos to build a sense of community and belonging. Such board meetings can rise to the level of the Holy Spirit's ability to do even the impossible.

The Community Of Faith

The Holy Spirit has formed and shaped our lives through the community of faith. We are the children of this community. The community of the Holy Spirit through the centuries has brought about the compilation, translation, canonization, and the transmission of the scriptures to the present time. The sacraments, hymns and liturgy are the results of community through the centuries. It is the Holy Spirit that convenes us as a congregation to hear the word of God. It is the Holy Spirit who opens our hearts and minds to receive anew God's self-disclosure as the living word.

The sermon is the product of community. It is the result of the prayers, support and the sharing of pastor and people together guided by the Holy Spirit that makes possible the sermon event. What kind of sermon would it be without this kind of heart-to-heart communication? Most assuredly it would be ineffective.

As a United Methodist minister I am given the privilege and authority by the community of faith to stand in the pulpit and proclaim the scriptures. It is the community that has confirmed and ordained me. A bishop of the then Methodist Church, Fred Pierce Corson, laid his hands upon my head and said, "Take thou authority to preach the gospel." The bishop did not act on his own, but was acting on behalf of the community. James Forbes, pastor of Riverside Church in New York City, reminds us that "the preaching event is an aspect of the broader work of the Spirit to nurture, empower, and guide the church in order that it may serve the kingdom of God in the power of the Spirit" (*The Holy Spirit and Preaching,* p. 19).

We are called to wholeness. We can never be completely whole in and of ourselves. We need each other. We are all wounded people and none of us has it all together. None of us can go it alone. As we experience the Holy Spirit in community, we also experience healing, togetherness and wholeness.

Our greatest experience of healing and wholeness as a community is realized in our celebration of the Eucharist. At the Lord's table our differences of race and culture are overcome as we find our unity in the body of Christ. Through the centuries the Christian community has practiced, celebrated, and perpetuated this single, common, communal meal. The presence of the Holy Spirit through the broken body of Christ and his shed blood speaks to our brokenness and emptiness with hope, meaning, and wholeness. At the Lord's table the Christian community arrives at its most sacred, most meaningful moment as community.

For Further Reflection And Study

1. Does Luke's description of the church in such supernatural phenomena have significance for the church today? In what way?

2. Why is Christian community essential? What role does the Holy Spirit play in forming community?

3. Is it possible to avoid conflict in the Christian community? How can it be a creative conflict?

4. What does it mean "to make the Christian community safe for diversity"?

5. How is the Christian community different than other communities?

6. What about the thesis, "The Holy Spirit leads believers to different conclusions about the same issue"?

7. Do you agree that, "The gifts of the Spirit are given essentially to strengthen the Christian community"?

8. Do we have a divided or a united Christian Church today?

Chapter Four

Are You Charismatic?

Fred Craddock, professor of Preaching at Candler School of Theology, Emory University, tells about an experience he had on the West Coast when he went to speak at a seminary. Just before his lecture a student stood up and said, "Before you speak, I need to know if you are Pentecostal." The room grew silent as the student quizzed Craddock in front of the class. He was quite taken back by the student's questioning and finally Craddock asked, "Do you mean do I belong to the Pentecostal Church?" "No," said the student, "I am asking you if you are Pentecostal." "Are you asking me if I am charismatic?" was Craddock's reply. The young man said, "I want to know if you are Pentecostal." "Do you mean do I speak in tongues?" Becoming somewhat irritated the student declared abruptly, "I want to know if you are Pentecostal." Finally Craddock confessed, "I don't know what your question is." The student replied, "Obviously, you are not Pentecostal," and left the room. I feel exactly like Craddock. When people ask me if I am a charismatic or a Pentecostal, I am not really certain I understand their question.

Charisma is a Greek word that means "a gift." In the New Testament it is defined as the "gifts of grace." A charismatic is a person who possesses the unique gifts and graces of the Holy Spirit.

Television commentators and newspaper reporters find charisma to be a useful word to describe an elusive quality of charm. When someone has a personal magnetism, a persuasive power, a capacity to excite, motivate, or inspire we refer to them as a charismatic individual. Peter F. Drucker in his book, *The New Realities,* warns us to beware of charisma.

He said today the desire for charisma is a political death wish. He points out that no century has seen more leaders with more charisma than our twentieth century. He goes on to say that never have political leaders done greater damage than the four giant charismatic leaders of this century: Stalin, Mussolini, Hitler, and Mao. However, his use of the term "charisma" is a very narrow and restricted use of the word, having no understanding of the New Testament use of the word in its relationship to the grace of God.

Any definition of charisma without reference to the Holy Spirit would be deficient in its usefulness for community. Charisma as defined by Drucker would be personality centered rather than grace centered, leading to arrogance. Arrogance would certainly be disruptive and a detriment to community.

Chrisma is a New Testament word. In the New Testament it is restricted to the writings of the apostle Paul. Outside of the New Testament it is not a common word. In the New Testament it is derived from the word *charis,* meaning grace. Grace is that little New Testament word containing all we know about the gospel. Grace is defined as "God's love in action." God's grace is the unmerited, unearned, undeserved goodness of God freely given to us. Anything that comes to your life under these terms is grace. Therefore, a chrisma is a gift of God that flows from God's grace. The whole basic idea of the word is that of a free and undeserved gift, something given to a man or woman unearned and unmerited, which comes from God's grace and could never have been achieved or attained by a person's own effort.

Defining A Charismatic

If someone would approach you and ask, "Are you a charismatic?" it would probably be in a different connotation than what we have been describing. They would be asking, "Do you have the gift of tongues?" The reason being, there are those Christians today who associate the presence of the Holy Spirit with the speaking in tongues. This is unfortunate, because it is the misuse of a good New Testament word. In the New Testament, *charismatic* is never restricted to such a narrow view or definition, but refers to all the gifts of grace freely given.

Therefore, if I ask you if you are a charismatic, I am not asking you if you speak in tongues. But in the New Testament sense of the word *charisma*, I am asking you, "Are you a person that is seeking to allow the Holy Spirit to direct your life with the Spirit's gifts and graces?" If so, then in the New Testament use of the word, you are a charismatic.

For too long we have associated the Spirit exclusively with a single spectacular gift. But everyone of us who looks to Christ as Lord has a charisma. The housebound or bedridden church member can exercise the charisma of prayer as any active committee chairperson can. If you are a Christian you have a charisma. Remember the words of Paul to Timothy, "I now remind you to stir into flame the gift of God which is within you." The goal of every church is to be a community of faith in which every member has stirred into flame the charisma God has given — whatever it is. Since charisma is a New Testament word let us consider the meaning of that word in that context and its significance for us today.

Gifts Of The Spirit

First, the charisma, the gifts of the Spirit are not for a few, but are for all who believe. The apostle declares, "To each is given the manifestation of the Spirit for the common good" (1 Corinthians 12:7). The work of the Holy Spirit in the life of the believer is not esoteric, private, or elitist, but rather for empowerment to serve others.

Since Jesus was "the man for others," so the gifts of the Spirit are not for self-satisfaction but for the service of others. He says to us, "Take my charisma and heal the sick, cleanse the leper, raise the dead, feed the hungry, visit the outcast, and cast out devils."

Who are these people of charisma? It is those who have the gift of prayer, those who organize and plan for mission and inspire others, those who sing in the choir, teach, visit the sick, those who stand by the alcoholic, the addict, the AIDS patient. The person of charisma is one who approaches the Christian life as a serious call to service and witness and whose presence is an inspiration to others. The Spirit-filled Christian is one who seeks to break down the walls and barriers that separate bringing healing, understanding, and wholeness in the name of Jesus.

The charismatic church is not a church which has a group of people who speak in tongues or outstanding personalities who attract attention, but the transformation of ordinary people in the Holy Spirit. A charismatic church is one that yields to the direction of the Holy Spirit and possesses a variety of gifts, who in their way, do their thing to the glory of God.

John Wesley talked about the scriptures and the gifts of the Spirit in regard to personal holiness. But he was quick to point out that the results were social holiness. The gifts of the Spirit are for others never for the few. Not only is the Holy Spirit the creator of community, but the gifts of the Spirit are to serve and strengthen the community.

Serving others is, after all, the whole purpose of spiritual gifts. "As each has received a gift, employ it for one another, as good stewards of God's varied grace" (1 Peter 4:10). To use the gifts of the Spirit for self would cause them to diminish, but using them for others would create a greater outpouring of God's spirit upon one's life. Our greatest satisfaction is not being served, but to serve.

Variety In The Gifts Of The Spirit

Second, there are varieties of gifts, but the same God inspires them all. God is a God of infinite variety. Here in Florida we do not have just palm trees, but there are over 100 different varieties of palms. I attended the International Orchid Show in Miami a few years ago and I discovered that there are hundreds of varieties of orchids. It was an awesome display of color and variety. Our God is a God of infinite variety.

Each of us is a unique individual. We have distinguishing characteristics of temperament and personality, as well as physical characteristics. As we become vessels of the Holy Spirit, the Spirit respects and enhances our uniqueness. The truth of the Spirit is expressed through human personality and the unique characteristics of personality are maintained.

We can see this expressed clearly in the scriptures. Abraham, Moses and Joseph were men who had very unique personal characteristics. Jeremiah, Ezekiel and Amos were prophets, but that is where their similarities ended. They were men of distinct uniqueness and individuality. The writers of the four gospels were men who possessed four distinct styles of writing. They were inspired by the Holy Spirit in their writings, but the uniqueness of their personalities is evident. The apostle Paul had a very distinctive style of writing that set him apart from all other New Testament writers. The Holy Spirit respects and enhances a person's uniqueness.

Varieties Of Religious Experience

There are varieties of religious experience. A congregation is made up of a group of people who have experienced the presence of God in their individual lives, in one way or another. As many people as there are in a congregation there are that many distinct religious experiences. Each member has come to God by a different road. Every religious experience has a history and the influences and factors that make up that history are different for each one. Although there are varieties of gifts and a variety of religious experiences that express these gifts we must keep in mind the apostle's admonition, "... there are varieties of gifts, but the same Spirit; and there are varieties of service, but the same Lord; and there are varieties of working, but it is the same God who inspires them all in every one" (1 Corinthians 12:4-6).

When it comes to the variety of gifts, Leonard Sweet has a marvelous story.

> *It is time for Thanksgiving dinner. The whole family is gathered around the table, waiting eagerly for the arrival of the fatted bird. In from the kitchen comes a steaming platter filled with turkey and all the fixings. Suddenly, the platter tips over and everything dumps onto the floor. Now watch how quickly all the spiritual gifts go to work. The prophet is usually the first one to speak. The Prophet: "Look what you've done! How are we going to eat? I warned you before . . ." The Giver: "Don't worry about anything. I'll just go out and buy some more meat at the nearest open market." The Servant: "There's no need to get excited. I'll have this mess wiped up in a minute and no one will ever know anything happened." The Teacher: "The reason why the platter dropped is that two-thirds of the turkey's weight was improperly positioned at the north end of the platter, causing the carrier to walk off-balance and trip on the rug." The Exhorter: "I see three things that we can learn from this experience . . ." The Merciful: "Don't feel badly. I've dropped many things myself over the years. Did I ever tell you how embarrassed I got . . . .?" The Administrator: "O.K., now, let's get organized. John, you go to the store. Mary, you find me some breadcrumbs . . ." The Sage: "God has a purpose in this disruption and disappointment." The Healer: "With a little cleaning up, this bird will be as good as new."*
> — New Life in the Spirit, p. 76f

To deal with this crisis they needed all the gifts. Where are you in this picture? What gifts of the Spirit would you bring to such a crisis situation? The gifts of each person will vary in regard to the function that he or she may perform. Some Christians yield to feelings of inferiority because they think that their spiritual gifts rank below the gifts of others. Those who may possess a more spectacular display of a gift may also cause others to feel that their gifts are inferior. Let me paraphrase Paul's words in 1 Corinthians 12: "There are no unimportant spiritual gifts. Be grateful for the gift God has given you. Don't seek to be a copy of someone else, but to be an original.''

The Necessity Of Love

When we talk about the gifts of the Holy Spirit we must move from the 12th to the 13th chapter of 1 Corinthians where the apostle declares, ''I will show you a more excellent way.'' He discusses faith, hope and love, but concludes that the greatest of all is love. Love is the sun around which revolves all the other gifts in the galaxy of the Holy Spirit. Without love the spiritual gifts are wasted and worthless. The world would have written another history of this century if the Pentecostal Church had spread love as they have spread speaking in tongues. Leonard Sweet believes that too many Christians are in the right book, 1 Corinthians, but the wrong chapter. We need to stop living in the 12th chapter and move to the 13th chapter, where we discover that love is the greatest gift of all (*New Life in the Spirit,* p. 81).

It is right to associate the lively, exciting, and the transforming phenomena in Christianity with the Holy Spirit. But it is a fallacy to identify the Holy Spirit exclusively with the miraculous and emotional, or with the speaking in tongues and ecstasy. We must remember that the Holy Spirit is the giver of a quiet ethical judgment, the giver of intellectual stimulation, and the giver of an ordered moral discipline. James Dunn points out in his extensive study of the Holy Spirit that the main thread that runs through it all is Jesus Christ. ''As the Spirit is the divinity of Jesus, so Jesus is the personality of the Spirit'' (*Expository Times,* Oct. 1982, p. 14). The test of the Holy Spirit in the charismatic congregation is the test of what is Christ-like.

> *For by one Spirit we are all baptized into one body —*
> *Jews or Greeks, slaves or free — and all were made to*
> *drink of one Spirit.* — 1 Corinthians 12:13

51

For Further Reflection And Study

1. What does it mean to be a charismatic Christian?

2. Define *charisma* as it is used in the New Testament.

3. What does it mean to say, "The gifts of the Spirit are not for a few, but for all who believe"?

4. What is the significance of 1 Corinthians 12:4-6 for today's church?

5. Why do the gifts of the Spirit sometimes become divisive in a congregation?

6. Is it a fallacy to always identify the Holy Spirit with the miraculous and emotional? Explain.

7. What do you think about James Dunn's comment, "The test of the Holy Spirit in the charismatic congregation is the test of what is Christ-like"?

Chapter Five

The Language Of The Spirit

What was the first gift of the Spirit to the church on Pentecost? It was the gift of tongues. It was the ability to communicate with one another. It was a language that transcended national and cultural barriers and brought about mutual understanding and unity.

A Spirit-filled church has a gift of tongues. It possesses a special language of the Spirit. It is a language that is identifiable and understandable by all. It is distinct in grammar, mood, accents, and idioms. A church of the Spirit speaks the language of the Spirit. What are the characteristics of the language of the Spirit?

An Informed And Understandable Language

First, the language of the Spirit is an intelligent and informed language. It is not an empty, mindless confusion of words and sounds that are unintelligible, but rather a knowledgeable and intelligent language.

On the day of Pentecost there was fresh power, energy and enthusiasm, and this is what we have come to regard as the signs of the Spirit. But, these were merely the external signs that something had happened, the effects which catch the eye. It is inevitable, with the coming of a new movement, that these are the things that capture our attention. But the New Testament seems to suggest that they do not make up the whole Pentecostal experience. These things were not the primary ingredients, but rather the by-products or fringe benefits of the experience. They were not the experience itself.

In Acts 2, the first gift of the Spirit appears to be the gift of tongues but the immediate result of that gift is preaching.

At Pentecost, preaching breaks out all over the place. The crowds are utterly amazed. Not because they are acting strangely: such a sight was not uncommon to the people in the first century. Rather, it was because these men and women were able to hear the great things that God had done being proclaimed in a language that they could understand. Therefore the uniqueness of Pentecost was that the church possessed the language of the Spirit that was an intelligent, knowledgeable, and understandable language for all to comprehend.

Now they were preachers, and this was something which the crowd could not see. They saw other dramatic, outward signs of the Spirit's manifestation. But the onlookers were not aware that the apostle's eyes had been opened to the truth of Christ. His teachings and the events of his life, which up to this point made little sense to them, have now come alive for them in a new way. Pentecost was a moment of disclosure. Things to them that had been familiar, but confusing and puzzling, began to fall into place and have meaning. Now faith really came alive. The promise that Jesus made to them, that the Holy Spirit would teach them all things, began to take on great significance. They were now able to speak of the great things of God in the language of the Spirit that others could understand.

We must never lose sight that the language of the Spirit is an informed language. Whenever knowledge increases, true religion is enhanced. A mindless faith dishonors, even blasphemes God. To close our minds to honest inquiry, study and knowledge would cause the language of the church to become garbled and unintelligible. A woman who was critical of John Wesley said to him, "Mr. Wesley, God can get along quite well without your scholarship." Whereupon Wesley replied, "True, madam, and God can get along quite well without your ignorance." If I were to have a patron saint it would be St. Francis. I have a statue of St. Francis in my study and there is a dove on his shoulder. Realizing that the dove is the symbol of the Holy Spirit it is as though the Holy Spirit is breathing the wisdom of God into his ear. Oh, that we would be listening to the knowledgeable, intelligent, and informative language of the Spirit.

A Reconciling Language

Second, the language of the Spirit is a reconciling language. The Holy Spirit among us causes us to speak a language that brings all things into harmony with God and with each other. The Spirit unifies as the Spirit diversifies. The Spirit promotes unity by preserving diversity. The presence of the Holy Spirit among us does not mean uniformity of method or the unanimity of thought. Such uniformity is dull and uncreative, whereas the Holy Spirit seeks to provide a unity that preserves diversity producing a community of growth, excitement and creativity.

Look at Acts 2:8-11:

> *And how is it that we hear each of us in his own native language? Parthians and Medes and Elamites and residents of Mesopotamia, Judea and Cappadocia, Pontus and Asia, Phrygia and Pamphylia, Egypt and the parts of Libya belonging to Cyrene, and visitors from Rome, both Jews and proselytes, Cretans and Arabians, we hear them telling in our own tongues the mighty works of God.*

This is a vivid description of diversity, people from all cultures, races and nations. Yet there was unity, because they had understanding. Each one heard and understood the mighty works of God. The miracle of Pentecost is the miracle of communication which is made possible by the reconciling language of the Spirit. In a previous chapter I shared the experience I had in a culturally and racially diverse congregation in Miami. On one Pentecost Sunday, because of the heterogeneous nature of the congregation I made this translation of Acts 2:8-12.

> *And how is it that we hear each of us in his own native language? Latins and Americans and Europeans and*

55

residents of North America, Puerto Rico and Granada,
Jamaica and the Dominican Republic, Cuba and Mont-
serrat, Antigua and the parts of the West Indies that be-
long to the Caribbean, and visitors from the United States,
both black and white, north and south, we hear them tell-
ing in our own language the mighty works of God.

I have a feeling that this is the way the church was intended to be.

The Holy Spirit creates community where it is safe to disagree. It is not safe to disagree in some parts of the world today. There are still closed societies with no freedom of expression. To deviate from the party line would mean imprisonment or death. Some churches require a uniformity of belief. In such churches you are required to accept the church's creedal statement without question in order to become a member. In other congregations you must agree with the preacher or leave. What a dull existence without the free exchange of ideas. How could the Holy Spirit be at work in a closed community?

In Acts 2 there seems to be a conflict that is genuine, creative, and yet peaceful which gives the appearance of life and vigor. The presence of the Holy Spirit in such a community makes the individual more alive, authentic and unique. The Spirit does not transform our "I's" into "We's," but turns our "I's" into more distinctive "I's." Leonard Sweet points out, "There will also be different opinions and many points of view in the church, even eternity. He finds it hard to picture Calvin and Wesley, Wagner and Dubussy, Hans Kung and John Paul II, dwelling together in heaven without disagreement. Conflict is a function of our freedom, a sign that we who have been created in the likeness of the triune God are developing and deepening that image" (*New Life in The Spirit*, p. 63). The language of the spirit is a reconciling language.

The Language Of Compassion And Concern

Third, the language of the Spirit is a language of compassion and concern. The word compassion contains the word passion, suggesting enthusiasm. The Holy Spirit moves over the slumbering coals of our lives producing a flame of exuberance, thrill, joy and action. This was certainly true for the disciples at Pentecost. This was remarkable because we had not seen them like this before. Prior to Pentecost they seemed confused and bewildered. At times they appeared frightened, uncertain and shaken. But now the Holy Spirit had opened their eyes to the truth of Christ, as he had promised, and his teachings came alive for them in a new way. Their timidity was transformed into boldness, their uncertainty into assurance that was characterized by joy and enthusiasm.

We must keep in mind that this new strength and vigor came to them because this new truth possessed them and it became the driving force in their lives. It is fatally easy to mistake the fringe benefits for the heart of the matter. In viewing the events of Pentecost we are tempted to see only power, joy and peace. But the power of Pentecost is only possible as we allow ourselves to be possessed by the Spirit of truth. We seek joy forgetting that joy is a by-product of our relationship with God. We seek peace forgetting that it is only the result of openness to God.

None of these things should be our prime objective. Our prayer at Pentecost should be for the Holy Spirit to work as the teacher, as the one who opens eyes that are closed, opens hearts that are unaware, and opens minds that are closed to truth. The disciples displayed new strength and vigor because this new truth had entered their hearts and became the driving force in their lives.

The language of the Spirit is the language of compassion. Compassion is love in action. In the New Testament it is the daring of Christ who not only speaks and teaches, but who dares to eat with publicans, meet with prostitutes, touch the polluted bodies of lepers and associate with the poor and rejected.

Compassion is the single-mindedness of the paralytic's four friends who risk their reputation and even their lives by lowering the paralytic through the roof so he may come into the healing presence of Christ. Compassion is Father Damien who went as a missionary to the leper colony on the island of Molokai. He addressed them as "you lepers." Then one day he addressed them as "we lepers." He ministered single-handedly to the spiritual and physical needs of 600 lepers, dressing their wounds, building them houses, and digging their graves, until finally his own leprosy rendered him helpless.

The Holy Spirit speaks a language of compassion in our church as seen by those who are doing something for the homeless in our community, those who have developed a program to feed the hungry, those who so graciously give of themselves to others in acts of humble service that are unknown to most of us. Our church will never create anything great or significant without compassion. The language of the Spirit is the language of compassion and concern.

Last summer, I joined a group of laity from our parish on a volunteer mission to the Dominican Republic. It was a remarkable experience. We were in a small village east of Santo Domingo called Las Tablitos. Here we worked on a building that will be used as a church, clinic and school. We worked side by side with the Dominicans. We ate their food and stayed in their homes.

On the last day we wanted to do something special. We decided to have a worship service and to invite the entire community. One member of our team got the best piece of wood he could find and crafted a cross for the front wall of the sanctuary. I realized that my limited Spanish would hinder me from communicating even though I had an interpreter. Therefore, I planned to have a communion service and so I could communicate to them through the sharing of the bread and the chalice.

We invited the people and they came, men, women and children crowding into the new building. Just prior to sharing the sacrament, a member of our team and the man who was to become the new pastor of this church together placed the cross on the wall. I started to sing, "On a hill far away stood an old rugged cross." The people recognizing the tune began to sing in Spanish as the cross was lifted up and placed on the wall. It was a very heart-rendering moment to say the least. I shared with them that the cross is the symbol of God's love through Christ for all people, in all places, at all times. Then I lifted the bread saying, "This is the body of Christ broken for you." And then lifting the chalice, "This is the blood of Christ shed for you. Come and feast upon the Lord by faith with thanksgiving."

They came. Those who had worked with us side by side in mixing mortar, carrying blocks, shoveling sand, putting in windows, hanging doors, and digging ditches came. The men had gone home and gotten their wives and children and they all came as we sang together the chorus "Alleluia" and together shared in the common meal at the Lord's table. I had never experienced such a celebration of the Eucharist as that moment together with those people in Las Tablitos. Following the service we shared greetings and warm embraces. A spirit of love and compassion prevailed. We wanted these people to know that God loved and cared for them and that there were people in the world who had compassion and concern for them. I am certain we got the message across. Just like the day of Pentecost, through our sharing together at the Lord's table we all heard "in our own tongues the mighty works of God." It was a great moment when together we spoke the language of the Spirit, a language of compassion and concern.

For Further Reflection And Study

1. What really happened in regard to language on the day of Pentecost? What significance does this have for us today?

2. What is meant by the statement, "The first gift of the Spirit to the church at Pentecost was the gift of tongues"? What was accomplished by this gift?

3. Describe the language of the Spirit as:

   a. an "informed language"

   b. a "reconciling language"

   c. as a language of "compassion and concern."

Chapter Six

Toward A More
Sensuous Christianity

In using the word "sensuous," I am not using the word in a carnal or bestial sense, but rather in a sensory sense. The experience of the Holy Spirit is sensuous in the sense that it is stimulating, inspiring, exciting and at times emotional. The apostle reminds us, "For the kingdom of God is ... joy in the Holy Spirit" (Romans 14:17).

When electricity was first introduced some Frenchmen wanted to know how fast electricity moves, so the abbot of a large monastery volunteered his monks for an experiment. They lined up 1,000 monks, each holding the hand of the monk next to him. Then an electrical current was applied to the first man in line. The result was that every one of the 1,000 monks jumped into the air at precisely the same time. You could draw three conclusions from this story. First, electricity moves with astonishing speed. Second, abbots in French monasteries in the eighteenth century had tremendous authority over their monks. Third, wouldn't it be wonderful today if 1,000 people in church could get excited enough to jump into the air at the same time?

As we focus on Pentecost and especially the Spirit's activity in today's world and in our lives, the Neo-Charismatic movement is a force to be reckoned with. Regardless of what one may think about their theology or motivation they have made religion exciting. They go to church and enjoy it. They sing hymns with enthusiasm like they believe the words. The Bible is so important to them that they even read and study it. Their lives are centered around Bible study, prayer meetings and outreach programs. There is a sense of euphoria about their overall religious experience.

I do not believe that God ever intended religion to be as dull as some people have made it. Leonard Sweet told about returning to his home church, the place where life for him had been exciting and where he received the call to ministry. He said the church of his homecoming was a different church: lifeless and corpse-cold. The pastor had settled in for a long winter's nap and he spoke as though the church was a casket for the eternal. He said, "I looked around at the handful of glassy-eyed youths, whose sole inspiration was coming from the stained-glass windows. Sunday morning meant for them the most painful hour of the week" (*New Life in the Spirit,* p. 44).

The story is told about a grandmother who had taken her grandson to the Sunday morning worship service. During the service the mind of the boy became restless and as he was looking around the sanctuary he spotted a bronze plaque on the wall. He asked his grandmother what the plaque stood for and she replied, "It lists the names of those who died in the service." The boy thought about that for a moment and asked, "Did they die in the morning or the evening service?" As Sweet reflected on that homecoming experience he wondered what would have become of his life, if he had come to associate the church solely with "bingo, bazaars, and bad sermons." I agree with his conclusion that we have failed to be informed by the Bible, which knows no other kind of church but a pentecostal church and no other Christian than a charismatic Christian.

Charismatic Renewal

In the established church the Spirit has become less the subject of experience and more the object of dogma. It is interesting that by the second century the church decided that the only channels of the Spirit were through the sacraments, thus confining the Spirit to the clergy and the priesthood. It would appear that the charismatic renewal is a reaction against the intellectualism of the religious establishment. The charismatic renewal has created a new life in the Spirit that at times is accompanied by the speaking in tongues which renders an immediate validation of the Holy Spirit's presence for the believer and is available to everyone regardless of social status, education or previous experience. This Neo-Pentecostal phenomenon transcends denominations, nations, cultures and promises direct access to the Holy Spirit. Is not this one of the basic aspects of the Holy Spirit in the Book of Acts? This charismatic renewal is seen as a lay people's movement to take religion out of the hands of the experts. It is a reaction against the lack of feeling in worship and through this rediscovery of emotions, dance, praise, and the senses, the new figure of the "sensuous Christian" is an indication of the spontaneity of our time.

When we talk about the Spirit of God and the kingdom of God it is more than just sermons. It is a question of demonstrating that we do indeed take seriously the business of letting the Spirit of God rule our lives as a church and as individuals. When outsiders observe the church are they aware that there is a spiritual power present in the life of a congregation? When strangers come among us do they sense the presence of a compassionate concern, as well as joy and enthusiasm? When I go to a football game I expect to be surrounded by football enthusiasts. If I go to a symphony concert I expect to be surrounded by music lovers. When people come to worship why shouldn't they be surrounded by enthusiasts for the kingdom of God, by God lovers? Several years ago when I stopped at the welcome station after entering the state of Virginia I was given a bumper sticker that read: "Virginia Is For Lovers." The church is for lovers and when people enter the fellowship of Christian worship they should be able to sense that love which is generated by the presence of God's spirit.

The Non-Rational And The Ecstatic

Personal experience reminds me that there are many liabilities that accompany this rising tide of emotion and feelings. The reality being that spiritual gifts lead to spiritual arrogance. Those who are high on the fumes of such religious ecstasy have, in Sweet's words, "a silliness and spookiness" in the way they describe the work of the Holy Spirit. Also, I realize that the apostles at Pentecost were overwhelmed by the charismata. It was an emotional and enthusiastic experience, at times ecstatic and illogical.

In our celebration of Pentecost we need to ask the questions, "What role did the non-rational and ecstatic play in Christian beginnings — and what role does it play in experiencing Christian life, being and worship today?" During my seminary years we were trained not to trust feelings or emotions. I am still somewhat of a rationalist seeking to express Christian experience, worship and social outreach in words that are sometimes oblivious to the fact that I am doing exactly that — reducing it all to a form of words and reason. I have come to realize that too much rationality can be as dangerous as too much non-rationality.

But the positive aspects of the charismatic awakening have been enormous. Future church historians will look upon this Neo-Pentecostalism as a seismic force that shook the foundations of twentieth century religious life. They will recognize that not since the eighteenth century Wesleyan revival has there been such a genuine stirring of the Spirit.

Personal Experience

The personal experience of the Holy Spirit was essential and central in the New Testament. The relationship to the Holy Spirit was not creedal, but experiential — an experience of tangible quality. James Dunn declares that there is an attitude of the Spirit in the New Testament with which modern Christianity is seemingly unfamiliar. (*Expository Times,* Oct. 1982, p. 8). He points out that in Romans 8 Paul does not say, "Because men are children of God therefore they are led by the Spirit," but rather, "It is those who are led by the Spirit who are the children of God." Again in Acts 19 Paul asks those at Ephesus whether they received the Spirit when they took their step of commitment. He expects an answer. As with all who claim to be disciples he expects that they will know whether they have received the Spirit or not. Christians are expected not merely to possess the Spirit, but to possess the Spirit "visibly and tangibly." This possession or lack of possession is the acid test of whether they are genuine disciples or not.

This same situation appears in John 3 where Jesus has his discussion with Nicodemus.

> ... it is spirit that gives birth to spirit ... The wind blows where it wills; you hear the sound of it, but you do not know where it comes from, or where it is going. So with everyone who is born of the spirit.
> — John 3:6b-8 NEB

This is to say that the Spirit is not always visible, and there is an element of mystery in the Spirit's coming. But you "will hear the sound of it." Although the wind itself is unseen, yet the effect of the wind is evident in the movement of the leaves, clouds and weather vanes. The same can be said about the wind or breath of the Spirit upon a person's life, the Spirit is visible from the effect that the Spirit has upon a human life. Where there is no sound, whistling, swirling or rustling, one can conclude that there is no wind present. Where men, women or congregations do not visibly show evidence of the Holy Spirit there is no Spirit.

The Neo-Charismatics give evidence of the Spirit's presence in their lives through their joy, excitement, and praise. Some back off from the Spirit because they cannot stand that much excitement. They are afraid that they may do something radical — such as make a personal witness of their faith, or tithe their income, or volunteer for a world or local mission project, or possibly go to worship and enjoy it, or get emotional about their religion, or experience a personal heartfelt religious experience that may change their lives forever. Fearing that such actions border on the emotional and fanatical they back off so as not to go overboard on religion.

Enthusiasm

If there is one thing we need it is enthusiasm. It is contagious. There is an enthusiasm about the Spirit that is highly contagious. This was true about the day of Pentecost. Jesus even referred to this in his promise prior to the Spirit's coming when he told the disciples, "When the Holy Spirit has come upon you; and you shall be my witnesses in Jerusalem and in all Judea and Samaria and to the end of the earth" (Acts 1:8). The effects of the Spirit in their lives is like the dropping of a stone in a pool of placid water with the continual motion of concentric circles that continue to reach out further and further. In the early church there was an infectiously contagious movement of the Spirit.

How is it that we can get excited about so many things except our religion? It is probably because there is nothing in our religion to get excited about. When religion is no more than part of one's respectability, something you can take or leave, having no connection between what one believes and how one lives, involving no personal commitment, making no demands on one's personal life or lifestyle, then how can anyone ever get excited over a religious experience like that?

In the Neo-Charismatic movement one is struck by the unaccustomed sight of worshippers who are glad they are there and having a good time. It is like the theme song on *Cheers:* "everybody knows your name and everybody is glad you came."

This movement is a return to experiential Christianity as in the early days of Methodism. Do not forget that Methodism was a lay movement reacting against the intellectualism, formalism, and spiritlessness of the established church. Now we are the established church and we have allowed ourselves to become intellectual, formal and spiritless. What these early Methodists came to cherish was not theories of atonement, doctrines, creeds about Christian theology and the Holy Spirit, but the experience of the Holy Spirit in their lives. Therefore, this new Pentecostal movement is nothing more than the old

Pentecostal movement that we as Methodists at one time enjoyed.

In such an experiential Christianity God is personal, where one can say not only that "Christ is the savior of the world, but he is my savior"; where one believes not only in the forgiveness of sins, but that one's sins are forgiven. The Holy Spirit is not only part of a Trinitarian theology, the Spirit is the indwelling, living presence of God in human life.

In our hymns our theology is set to music. Early Methodism was known for its enthusiastic singing. They could sing John Newton's "Amazing Grace" with feeling because they were wretched, they were lost, they were blind. It had meaning because they were the recipients of such an amazing grace. A favorite hymn of these early Methodists was Charles Wesley's "O for a thousand tongues to sing my great Redeemer's praise." And when they came to the second stanza, "He breaks the power of cancelled sin and sets the prisoner free," they would sing it with joy and feeling saying, "I am the prisoner that God has set free!" When experiencing such forgiveness, such liberty of heart and soul, it is something that one can sing about with enthusiasm.

Enthusiasm Has It Liabilities

Some of Paul's chief headaches were caused by some of the enthusiastic factions, particularly at Corinth. From 1 Corinthians 1:18 to 4:21 Paul confronts some of the Corinthian Christians who describe themselves as "the spiritual ones." They had achieved a higher plane of spirituality, they knew a higher wisdom, and they even despised the low level Christianity of Paul, among others.

In 1 Corinthians, there were those whom Paul described as possessing a superior knowledge in order to justify their action that was selfish and inconsiderate to those who did not share the same insights.

Every pastor has had to deal with those "spiritual elite" Christians described by Paul in 1 Corinthians who are seeking one religious high after another. They are always informing their pastor about their latest religious experience, which usually takes place in another church. They are often super-critical of the church's program because it falls short of their concept of being "spiritual," whatever that means. They usually end up sending their pastor a letter informing him that they are not being "fed spiritually" and they are going to transfer to a more "spiritual church." They are playing the game of "musical churches" and keep asking the question, "Spirit, spirit, who's got the spirit?"

Nevertheless, there is that genuine personal experience of the Holy Spirit which brings the living presence of Christ into human life which makes religion exciting.

For Further Reflection And Study

1. What is meant by the statement that "in the established church the Spirit has become less the subject of experience and more the object of dogma"?

2. What role does the "non-rational" and the "ecstatic" play in religious experience? What about enthusiasm?

3. What are the negative aspects of the charismatic renewal?

4. What are the positive aspects of the charismatic renewal?

5. What particular problems do the "spiritually elite" present the pastor?

6. Describe early Methodism as an enthusiastic lay movement with emphasis on personal experience.

7. Describe the meaning of the statement, "O Lord, either enlarge the vessel or withdraw thy Spirit."

Chapter Seven

The Promise Of The Spirit

As a mainline church we have been told to the point of weariness what is wrong with us. Many articles have been written about the demise of the mainline churches with their dwindling membership and attendance. Someone has figured out mathematically that if the United Methodists continue to lose members at the present rate, the last Methodist will leave the face of the earth in the year 2037. This is a very sobering thought.

The Dilemma Of Decline

To borrow a line from Dickens, these are, for the mainline Protestants, the "worst of times." The mainline churches in the early times of this century were used to vitality, growth, and widespread influence and popularity. Currently, they are experiencing severe decline. Martin Marty tells us that American religion now has a new map. And what is mapped is a massive realignment of American religious demography; a vast earthquake has shifted the so-called mainline denominations from the center to the margin of American religious life (*A Nation of Behavers,* University of Chicago Press, 1986). It is not only a margin of numbers but of vitality and influence. He points out that now occupying the new center are large, rapidly growing, aggressive and politically and religiously conservative Protestant denominations. It is not uncommon to find huge religiously conservative bookstores in large shopping malls and learn that conservative seminaries count their enrollment by the thousands instead of the hundreds. In the wake of such rapid and expansive growth by conservative churches, the mainline churches have experienced the loss of national and local visibility and influence, forced to the slippery slopes of decline in numbers and vitality.

The real danger confronting the mainline churches is the temptation to reach out and grab anything that might offer any glimmer of hope and relief. Edward Farley in his article, "The Modern Element in Protestantism" (*Theology Today,* July 1990, p. 131), points out the real dangers of such temptations. "Communities are like individual human beings in the sense that times of decline, uncertainty, insecurity, and threat are times of greatest temptation. When threatened with harm, extinction, or even change, we human beings will latch on to all sorts of ideologies, worldviews, demagogues, authorities, and institutions which we think may save us. Times of peril and insecurity are times of idolatries and absolutisms" (p. 133). The mainline churches, staggered by losses, now begin to envy religious movements that glitter with power and slick success and wonder whether to imitate them.

It is the fact of our times, that churches that do not hesitate to make absolute claims about themselves and their interpretations, who offer certainties, who make unabashed and even manipulative use of the media have experienced substantial growth. Farley points out that religions that develop specific pieties and claim the very will of God and make absolute claims for their traditions and institutions do well. But he goes on to ask a most crucial question, "Are we in the business of religion?" Then he concludes that our calling is not to religion, but to faithfulness. It is not to growth and success, but to witness to the gospel. One thing is evident: our destiny as mainline churches does not lie along the path of retreat from modernism nor in attempts to hug the right side of the theological road. But as Farley goes on to point out, critical modernism alone has never been a sufficient rallying point. We must go beyond the negative critical principle to affirm the positive, namely, that "God redeems, transforms, and empowers in and through the earthen vessels of the creaturely, the cultural, the historical."

How do Protestant mainline churches regain their vitality? Where in all of this is the promise of the Holy Spirit? What about the Holy Spirit's promise of power, to make possible a strong witness, to give guidance, and to lead into new things? Pentecost bears witness to the church's potential. It is good for us to know about the sociological and theological reasons for the decline in our mainline churches. However, it is disastrous if we become paralyzed through discouragement. The situation is more like that in Ezekiel's vision of the valley of dry bones. Pentecost comes with a promise of new life and these dry bones can live again. This is the encouraging and challenging promise of Pentecost.

Although there may be few who seem to hold out much hope for the mainline churches, we must not lose sight of the potential of the Holy Spirit to bring new life. It has happened before and it can happen again. The Spirit acknowledges human weakness and paradoxically it glories in that weakness, because it is in weakness that the power of God is manifest. The word of the Lord to Paul was, "For my power is made perfect in weakness" (2 Corinthians 12:9). This is the message of Pentecost.

The Promise Of Power

First, look at Acts 1:8:

> *But you shall receive power when the Holy Spirit has come upon you; and you shall be my witnesses in Jerusalem and in all Judea and Samaria and to the end of the earth.*

This promise about the Spirit is from Jesus. The promise is the promise of *power*. To understand the nature of this power look at the Greek word that is used for power in the text. It is the noun *dunamis*, from which we derive our word for dynamic, dynamite and dynamo. This seeks to express the magnitude of this power. This power in the life of the Christian and in the church is unlimited. It is an inexhaustible source of power. It has been suggested that all we need in the church to accomplish our goals is money. Never. What we need is the Holy Spirit. Here is a limitless source of power that can do far more than mere money could ever do. The ministry of the church is not dependent on money but the Spirit. Money is limiting and confining, whereas the Spirit knows no bounds and can accomplish the impossible.

The promise of power in this passage in Acts 1:8 is the power to be an effective witness for Christ. That witness was to operate in the manner of an ever widening series of concentric circles, beginning in Jerusalem, where Pentecost was experienced, and extending to the ends of the earth. The following account in the book of Acts shows how this power was a mighty factor in their lives. They were men and women with a message to proclaim, come what may. "For we can not keep from speaking about what we have seen and heard" (Acts 4:20 NRSV).

Every Christian is called to be Christ's witness. Not only do we have the call and the commission to be witnesses, but we too have the promise that is attached to it. The Holy Spirit was the driving force and influence behind the church's ability to witness to Christ. It was the work of the Holy Spirit that brought about the power to convert this small band of ordinary, weak, and fearful men in Jerusalem into a force of fearless evangelists who "turned the world upside down." The power of the Holy Spirit is promised to the church in every age to enable the church to fulfill its mighty task of witnessing to her Lord to the ends of the earth.

Do not underestimate what the power of the Holy Spirit can do. Look at the incredible things that happened in Acts. There was healing, the restoring of relationships and the overcoming of racial and cultural barriers which appeared insurmountable. Do not underestimate the power of the Spirit in your life. Here is a boundless source of power to meet every human need. I went to the hospital to visit an older member of the parish and to my surprise I discovered she was listed as being in the maternity ward. I told the attendant at the desk that there must be some mistake and I asked her if she would call the nurse's station to see if the woman was there. To my surprise the nurse said she was there. When I arrived at the lady's room she said to me, "Are you surprised to see me here?" I told her that I was and she went on to explain that the test she was having could only be performed in that department of the hospital. As I was leaving she said to me with a twinkle in her eye, "Don't you underestimate this 82-year-old woman!" No matter how burdened or despondent we become we must not underestimate what the Holy Spirit can do.

On the day of Pentecost the disciples received something that they never had before — power. Prior to this experience they were so timid, uncertain, stammering and confused. Incredibly Acts 2:14-17 records,

> *But Peter, standing with the eleven, lifted up his voice and addressed them, "Men of Judea and all who dwell in Jerusalem, let this be known to you, and give ear to my words. For these men are not drunk, as you suppose, since it is only the third hour of the day; but this is what was spoken by the prophet Joel: 'And in the last days it shall be, God declares, that I will pour out my Spirit upon all flesh . . .' "*

The disciples had preached before, but never with such force, power or persuasion. Never had they experienced such results.

> *So those who received his word were baptized, and there were added that day about three thousand souls. And they devoted themselves to the apostles' teaching and fellowship, to the breaking of bread and the prayers.*
> — Acts 2:41-42

This sense of power that came to the disciples was the ability to do and to accomplish. This was surely the way the church was meant to be. Vigorous and flexible. These were the years before it became fat and short of breath through prosperity and muscle-bound by over-organization. Remember that Methodism began as a lay movement, spirit-filled, expressive, spontaneous, vocal, and exciting, and this is the way Methodism was meant to be.

We are no longer a movement, but now we are an institution. We are encumbered with all the problems that beset institutions; the maintaining of the institution, caring for the survival of the institution, becoming preoccupied with budgets, agendas, and strategy. In the process the power and presence of the Spirit has been weakened. J. B. Phillips in his Introduction to his translation of Acts, titled *The Young Church in Action,* says of the apostles that they did not make acts of faith; they believed. They did not say their prayers; they prayed. They did not hold conferences on medicine; they healed the sick.

You may consider these early Christians in Acts uncomplicated and naive by modern standards. However, you would have to admit that they were open on the God-ward side in a way that is unknown to us today. First, the promise of the Spirit was the promise of power.

The Promise Of Guidance

Second, the promise of the Spirit is the promise of guidance.

When the Spirit of truth comes, he will guide you into all the truth; for he will not speak on his own authority, but whatever he hears he will speak, and he will declare to you the things that are to come. — John 16:13

When present the Holy Spirit will lead. Life in the Spirit is never static, calm, or status quo. The presence of the Spirit means life, movement, activity, for that is the nature of the Spirit. Look at Jesus' words in John 3:

The wind blows where it wills, and you hear the sound of it, but you do not know whence it comes or whither it goes; so it is with every one who is born of the spirit. — John 3:8

76

The Bible is a record of the unending march of God's purpose through history. God calls us to be Spirit-led and to follow God. The work of the Spirit is to prod, move and inspire men and women to be active participants in the kingdom of God. God drives Abraham from the ease and comfort of Haran declaring, "Go from your country and your kindred and your father's house to the land that I will show you. And I will make you a great nation, and I will bless you . . ." (Genesis 12:1-2).

The disciples left the comforts of home and families to follow Jesus. They left their nets dangling over the sides of their fishing boats as they responded to Jesus' call, "Come and follow me and I will make you fishers of men." When Jesus prays for his disciples in John 17 he does not pray for their ease and comfort but he prays, "As you have sent me into the world, so I have sent them into the world."

Philip Schaff reminds us that on Pentecost the disciples received their baptism, confirmation, and ordination, all in one, for they received no other. To them it was the great inspiration which enabled them to be authoritative teachers of the gospel by tongue and pen. What previously had been confusing and mysterious to them (there were many things about Jesus' life they did not comprehend), now became clear and full of meaning for them. The Holy Spirit revealed to them the person and work of the Redeemer in light of his resurrection and exaltation, and took full possession of their minds and hearts.

The disciples were illuminated, controlled, and directed by the Holy Spirit. The manifestation of the Spirit's power was manifested in utterances that broke through the confines of ordinary speech and burst out in ecstatic laughter of praise and thanksgiving. Schaff declares, "It was the Spirit himself who gave them utterance and played on their tongues, as on new tuned harps, unearthly melodies of praise. It was the first *Te Deum* of the newborn church" (*History of the Christian Church,* Vol. 1, p. 230f).

77

Francis Giovanni was the son of a rich clothing merchant in southern Italy. He was a gallant, high-spirited young man, free-wheeling and wealthy. One day he attended mass at Portiuncula, a few miles south of his hometown of Assisi. It was here that Francis heard the words, "Preach, the kingdom of God is at hand, heal the sick, cleanse the lepers, cast out devils. Provide neither silver nor gold, nor brass in your purses." Throwing away his staff, purse and shoes he made these commands the rule of his life and he gathered other companions around him and he became known as St. Francis of Assisi, and his group, the Franciscans. In 1210 Francis went to receive the blessing of Pope Innocent III upon his group. The pope seeking to test his sincerity said, "Go, brother, go to the pigs, to whom you are more fit to be compared than to men, and roll with them and to them preach the rules you have so ably set forth." Francis obeyed and returning to the pope said, "My Lord, I have done so." The pope then gave his blessing and told him to go and preach repentance. At this time there occurred one of the most remarkable episodes of Francis' career. He entered into marriage with poverty. He called poverty his bride and remained devoted to her with the devotion of a knight. With only a simple robe tied with a cord, barefoot, he set out on a lifelong ministry devoted to the poor. The Spirit of the Lord was upon him.

The Spirit drove Luther out of the monastery in 1517 and it was like striking a match in a tinderbox, touching off a firestorm of revival and reformation that spread throughout Europe. Wesley was driven by the Spirit out of the established pulpits of England which he loved to the open air of Bristol where he preached to the coal miners the unsearchable riches of Christ, bringing an unprecedented spiritual awakening.

The same Spirit is driving us today to move out of our complacency and ease into the exciting stream of the Spirit's activity in our world. Is it not possible that God is driving this generation into the wilderness away from the temples and the traditions, away from the ideals which have become idols, forcing us to be a pilgrim people? It is not easy for us to grasp this, or to gain any comfort from it, because we think of security in the certain terms of institutions and temples. We like our churches to be Gothic, granite-like, to be a solid rock in a world of flux and change, a place of refuge amid the milieu of unsettledness, a place where things will never change but remain the same. But it is not the church but Christ "who is the same yesterday, today and forever." If we demand that the church or anything else be "the same yesterday, today and forever," we shall be disappointed. We scan the wilderness for something stable. We long for a simple Gospel that would make no demands on thought, reason or lifestyle, but it's merely a mirage. If we accept the promise of the Spirit, who will lead us into all truth, such a journey will be one of constant challenge demanding change and flexibility. We must never lose sight that it is "the truth that sets us free" and the challenge of change is the price of freedom.

There is a suspicion that certain things we have known especially in areas of unquestioned authority such as education, economics, political and military power are today suspect. A variety of scholars are calling attention to the prospect that Enlightenment modes of power and Enlightenment modes of knowledge are at the end of their effective rule among us. (See Brueggemann's *Hopeful Imagination: Prophetic Voices in Exile*.) We are children of the Enlightenment which has brought us enormous gifts of human reason, freedom and possibility. Although we would not want to relinquish these gifts, they have come with high cost resulting in the concentration of power in monopolistic ways, often without ever being criticized. There are those who see the Spirit at work in the transforming of our world in the rise of Third World nations and in the emergence of the variety of liberation movements. The fear is that the church has been so fully meshed in the dominant values of our culture that freedom for action is difficult. The blending of the Christian faith with our culture has resulted in the church losing its prophetic voice.

The Spirit Leads Us To The Future

The Spirit promises to guide us into truth. There are new dreams in our world of justice and equity. Bob Dylan's words of the '60s seem relevant, "The answer, my friend, is blowing in the wind, the answer is blowing in the wind." The Holy Spirit is leading us into the future, transforming old structures and bringing new life in the Spirit. The promise of the Spirit is the promise of the future. Do not believe the words of the doomsayer and those who have brought out their dispensational charts seeking to convince us by their apocalyptic timetables that the rapture is upon us. These are exciting days and the Spirit is leading us into new things. This is all part of the guidance of the Spirit who leads and guides us to all truth.

This brings to mind Isaac Watts' hymn which used to be sung in Methodist campmeetings and now is in the new United Methodist Hymnal.

> *Then let our songs abound, and every tear be dry; we're marching through Emmanuel's ground to fairer worlds on high. We're marching to Zion, beautiful, beautiful Zion; we're marching upward to Zion, the beautiful city of God.*

The promise of the Spirit is the promise of the future. We are like Abraham as described by the writer of Hebrews, "For he looked forward to the city which has foundations, whose builder and maker is God" (Hebrews 11:10).

Thank God for the promise of the Spirit. The Spirit brings us a new surge of power to keep our optimism alive, to maintain our enthusiasm, to see clearly our responsibilities, and to recognize our potential. The Holy Spirit helps us to take bold and drastic action. We do not lack for opportunities, opportunities abound; but we need the power of the Spirit to give us the courage to make decisions that will mobilize us into action.

The promise of the Holy Spirit is the promise of power. It is the promise that the Spirit will lead and guide us into all truth. The Spirit leads us into the future, a future for which we do not need to be afraid, because "it is the Spirit himself bearing witness with our spirit that we are the children of God" (Romans 8:16).

For Further Reflection And Study

1. What are the reasons for the decline of the mainline churches?

2. What is your response to the statement that "God is not calling us to religion or success, but to be faithful witnesses to the gospel"?

3. How are the mainline churches to regain their vitality? What role does the Holy Spirit play in this process?

4. Define the promise of the Spirit as:

   a. the promise of power

   b. the promise of guidance

   c. the promise to lead to the future.

5. What do you think about the statement that religious experience is uncommon in the church today? Define "religious experience."

Chapter Eight

The Scope Of The Spirit

How is the power of the Holy Spirit within the Christian community related to divine activity in the world as a whole? Does the wind of the Spirit that blows within the church blow elsewhere in the world? There are those who almost instinctively sense that the Spirit is moving about in all levels of human activity seeking to unlock many doors and seeking to resolve many of our human dilemmas. In John 3:8 Jesus talks about the wind (pneuma) as the Spirit and that the wind "blows where it wills." This suggests that the Spirit moves freely in human affairs, unknown, unseen, and at times mysterious. Thus, the most important question of all is: Where is the Holy Spirit now working? These are fair questions for us to consider.

Leonard Sweet asks if it is appropriate to consider if God had the same interest in George Washington and his tattered army who took on England in the struggle for independence as for Moses and the crossing of the Red Sea? Is the Holy Spirit at work in the Bill of Rights as well as the Beatitudes; in Hemingway and Sandburg as well as Henri Nouwen and Frederick Buechner; in Spielberg as well as C.S. Lewis; in the White House as well as in Riverside Church or Pasadena Community Church?

The Wind Of The Spirit

The Old Testament authors without hesitation compared the Spirit of God with the wind. In the Hebrew the same term is used for both the Spirit and the wind. The word *ruach* meant breath. It meant the breath of life as well as the desert wind that at times blew violently across the desert.

This is illustrated by the incident that happened in 587 B.C. The Babylonians leveled the city of Jerusalem and destroyed the temple. They carried the Israelites off into exile and this was the beginning of what is called the Babylonian captivity. Walter Brueggemann in *Hopeful Imagination*, declares that 587 B.C. is the most important date in the Old Testament. He said for Israel it was a time of *relinquishment* and *reception*. Relinquishment in the sense that it was the end of the known world for Israel. The city and temple are destroyed. It is a time of letting go. Things will never be as they were. At the same time it was a moment for reception, to receive the new world that is given by God through the prophets. This new world will be nothing like the old world.

The Breadth Of The Spirit

From the time of the patriarchs, Abraham, Isaac, Jacob, and even Moses, they all felt that God was their God. They had exclusive rights on God. God fought their battles. They were God's chosen people and God was their God.

The Babylonians, under the direction of Nebuchadnezzar, destroyed Jerusalem and the temple and in humility the Israelites were carried off to a distant, strange land. There were those who raised their voices saying, "God has been defeated!" How else could the Israelites interpret those events? God failed them. Yahweh was defeated and a more powerful god than Yahweh had prevailed.

Jeremiah was the prophet at the time the Babylonians conquered the city. He said, "No one has defeated Yahweh. God has delivered the Israelites into the hands of the Babylonians. Babylon is God's instrument and Nebuchadnezzar is God's servant." Jeremiah seeks to reassure the people that the Spirit is working through the secular and political forces of their day to accomplish God's purpose. This is a new concept for them. Is it possible for a king and a nation who has no knowledge of God to become the instruments of God? Jeremiah said to the people, "Babylon has crushed Jerusalem and destroyed the temple, not because God is weak, but because Israel has been unfaithful to the covenant of Yahweh."

This is a remarkable moment in Old Testament history. Second Isaiah, who is a contemporary of Jeremiah, is the first Old Testament writer to insist that there is one God who rules the entire world. God declares, "I am the Lord, and there is no other, besides me there is no God" (Isaiah 45:5).

The Scope Of The Spirit

Do you see the scope of the Spirit here? The Spirit of God is active even in the lives of people and nations who have no knowledge of the Spirit. Even they can become the instruments of God's purpose. These events appeared chaotic and out of control, and that is exactly how the Babylonian's plundering must have appeared to Israel, but it all seemed so different after listening to Jeremiah and Isaiah. God is in control. Amid this quiet desperation the words of the prophets changed everything. All of this, which appeared as chaotic to Israel, Jeremiah said, was under the control and direction of the Spirit of God.

In the New Testament Jesus revealed the scope of the Spirit when he said to Nicodemus, "Listen to the wind. Nicodemus, the Spirit of God is just like that — invisible yet unmistakable, impalpable yet full of power. Listen to the wind."

What Jesus is saying to Nicodemus is that there is a constant, relentless movement of the Spirit. Never has there been a time, never a moment, when the Spirit of God has not been actively at work. James Stewart, in *The Wind of the Spirit,* points out that although there was a burst of a mighty rushing wind on Pentecost, it was but the identical power that had been in Jesus and now was forever inseparable from Jesus. From that moment until this, "the wind blows" — sometimes a gentle breeze, sometimes a judgment hurricane, sometimes a gentle voice in the moment of meditation and prayer, and sometimes a fierce tornado. But always is the Spirit at work.

The Sovereign Freedom Of The Spirit

Jesus not only said that the Spirit blows, but the Spirit "blows where it wills." There is a sovereign freedom of the Spirit. How many times have we in the church tried to institutionalize and domesticate the Spirit or restrict the Spirit's movement? This is the perennial temptation of institutional religion. We are constantly tempted to feel that our way is the only way, and we become impatient with others. But the Spirit always seems to upset our logical schemes and best laid plans. What audacity on our part to tell the Spirit where to work, what people, sect or group to become involved with, or to draw the lines circumscribing the Spirit's activity.

In Jesus' day there were those, the very followers of Jesus, who built their walls of partition and exclusiveness. But on the day of Pentecost, with a startling crash the walls of exclusiveness came tumbling down. Stewart points out, "This is the sovereign freedom of the Holy Spirit. There is no citadel of self and sin that is safe from him, no unbelieving cynic secure beyond his reach. There is no ironclad bastion of theological self-confidence that is immune, no impregnable agnosticism he cannot disturb into faith, no ancient ecclesiastical animosities he cannot reconcile .... This is the glory of Pentecost" (p. 14).

So Jesus said to Nicodemus,

> *The wind blows where it chooses,*
> *and you hear the sound of it,*
> *but you do not know where it comes from*
> *or where it goes.*   — John 3:8 NRSV

In this conversation with Nicodemus, Jesus is saying some very important things to us about the scope of the Spirit. As the wind blows it affirms the ceaseless, unrelenting movement of the Spirit among us. Since the wind blows where it wills, there is a sovereign freedom of the Spirit which cannot be controlled by human or institutional limitations. As the wind blows where it chooses and we hear the sound, this is the indisputable evidence of the Spirit's activity. There are those unmistakable signs that reveal to us that the power of the Spirit is at work among us. Since the wind blows and you cannot tell where the Spirit comes from or where the Spirit is going, this affirms the unpredictability of the Spirit. It is this quality of the Holy Spirit that makes the Spirit's presence so dynamic among us. One is never quite certain where the Spirit is leading us.

The Spirit's Activity Today

What about the Spirit's activity in today's world? Norman Pittenger has suggested that wherever there is a concern for justice, truth, and love — there the Spirit of God is at work. Pittenger insists that no one is devoid of the Holy Spirit. No one is without Luther's or Calvin's "common grace," Wesley's "prevenient grace," or George Fox's "inner light." Pittenger points out that God's Spirit is at work in this world in every place and in every person as expressed in John 9, "The true light that enlightens every man was coming into the world." I realize that Pittenger is somewhat of a generalist in regard to the Holy Spirit, yet there is reasonable truth about his understanding of the scope and range of the Holy Spirit within the world and within our lives.

The Spirit's Activity In Personal Life

This has meaning for us personally. In whatever location one seeks to do ministry — this is your cosmos, this is your world. My world of activities and relations happens to be St. Petersburg. For those within my parish this is where we build our relationships. It is here that we experience reality and seek to solve the problems of life. This is where we raise our families, conduct our business and build our associations. What we do here is important to God and we seek to be guided by the Holy Spirit in our activities. Our ministry in St. Petersburg is within the scope of the Holy Spirit's activity within the entire world.

What does this mean to us here in this city? It means that God is concerned with the people of our city. God is concerned that every family has food on their table, has shelter to live in, has medical care, has employment, and that each one's human rights are protected regardless of culture or race. This is the will of God for our community. Where there is any effort to accomplish these things — there is the Spirit of God assisting, inspiring, strengthening, and approving. The scope of the Spirit's activity is broad enough to include every human activity.

This also applies to our personal lives. Where is there evidence of the Holy Spirit in your personal life? How do you know that the Spirit leads and directs your life? The apostle declared in Romans 8:16, "It is the Spirit himself bearing witness with our spirit that we are the children of God." If we are the children of God, led by the Spirit, would it not be a logical conclusion that all things are then controlled, directed, interpreted, and integrated by the Spirit within our lives?

The Comfort Of The Spirit

The apostle went on to declare, "We know that in everything God works for good with those who love him, who are called according to his purpose" (Romans 8:28). I must admit that I do not always see this happening. I see things transpiring in human life that seem to have no rhyme or reason about them. They do not seem to be within the scope or the purpose of the Spirit. Some events seem to have no purpose, other than a destructive purpose. They do not seem to fit into the pattern of life. There are some pieces in the puzzle of life that just do not seem to fit. The more you seem to force them and try to make them fit, the more out of place they become. They seem to be beyond the scope of God's spirit.

There is a magnificent story in the Book of Genesis about Joseph and his brothers. Joseph's brothers were jealous of him. They grew to hate him and they wanted to get him out of their family by whatever means possible. The scriptures tell us that

Jseph's brothers "conspired to kill him." Their thoughts were evil and their deeds were evil. They sold their brother into slavery and he was carried off by slave merchants to Egypt. Many years later when his brothers came to Egypt, desperate for food, they came before Joseph, who was now Secretary of State for Pharaoh. They did not recognize him but he recognized them. Joseph looked them in the eye and said, "You meant evil against me; but God meant it for good ..." (Genesis 50:20).

What about a terrorist who places on an airplane a bomb that would cause the death of hundreds of passengers? What about an insidious racial policy devised and enforced by racist politicians that condemns millions of people to poverty, pain and anguish for decades? It could be said of them as Joseph said of his brothers, "They meant to do these things for evil." There are human actions that seem to have evil intent. What is the scope of the Spirit in the midst of such human suffering?

We must not forget about the freedom of human choice and its consequences. Men and women have the choice to choose evil. Joseph's brothers chose to do evil to their brother. God did not force them to do it. The terrorist chose to place that bomb on that Pan Am flight. God did not force him to do it. Those members of parliament who voted for apartheid in South Africa in 1948 did so with evil intent toward the black members of their country. That was an evil choice with far-reaching consequences. God is not responsible for everything that happens to us. Individuals and nations must bear the responsibility for their decisions.

No One Is Beyond The Scope Of The Spirit

What is the scope of the Spirit in this aspect of human life and suffering? My colleague Jim Harnish in his book, *Journeys with the People of Genesis*, makes this statement,

The good news is that while there may be circumstances over which God does not have absolute control and

"things" that God does not cause, there is no thing that God cannot turn into good. God may not be the author of all things, but God is the master of all things. There is no event, no experience of human life, that God cannot somehow weave into the tapestry of God's good purpose for us. — p. 122f

Just this way Jeremiah declared to the Israelites that nations and kings that had no knowledge of God became the instruments of God, carrying out God's purpose. Therefore, God can use all things for our good. This would involve even things and people of evil intent.

Ultimately, we can go back to Romans 8:28 and declare that "all things work together for good" with two qualifications — for those who love God and are called to God's purpose. Out of the mystery of divine grace God can take that which happens to us and weave it into the "tapestry of God's good purpose for us." There is tremendous breadth to the scope of the Spirit within our lives, to the extent that no place is out of bounds of God's love and care!

The writer of Psalm 139 sensed the broad scope of the Spirit activity among us when he wrote:

> *Whither shall I go from thy Spirit?*
> *Or whither shall I flee from thy*
> *presence?*
> *If I ascend to heaven, thou art there!*
> *If I make my bed in Sheol, thou*
> *art there!*
> *If I take the wings of the morning*
> *and dwell in the uttermost parts of*
> *the sea,*
> *even there thy hand shall lead me*
> *and thy right hand shall hold me.*

For Further Reflection And Study

1. Does the wind of the Spirit that blows in the church blow elsewhere?

2. Is it possible that the Holy Spirit is active in the lives of people and nations who have no knowledge of the Spirit? If so, where is this happening today?

3. Comment on Norman Pittenger's statement that "wherever there is a concern for justice, truth and love — there is the Spirit of God at work."

4. How do you respond to the statement that "There is *no* thing that God cannot turn into good. God may not be the author of all things, but God is the master of all things"?

5. Where is the Holy Spirit now at work?

Chapter Nine

The Holy Spirit
As The Dove Of Peace

The symbol of the descending dove has meant for the Christian community both the coming of the Holy Spirit and the symbol of peace. As we have seen, the community of the Holy Spirit is a creative and diverse community, yet a community where peace prevails characterized by openness and freedom, as well as, togetherness and unity. The words in John 14 tie together the concept of both the coming of the Holy Spirit and Jesus' desire for peace.

> *But the Advocate, the Holy Spirit, whom the Father will send in my name will teach you everything, and remind you of all that I have said to you. Peace I leave with you; my peace I give to you. I do not give to you as the world gives. Do not let your hearts be troubled, and do not let them be afraid.* — John 14:26-27 NRSV

A Shalom Community

The Holy Spirit desires peace. This was true from the beginning chapter of Genesis, where the Spirit of God hovered over the formless void of the earth bringing order, light, and life to the overall view of the Bible where the scriptures' central vision is that all of creation is one. Walter Brueggemann in *Living Toward a Vision* declared that in the community of faith in Israel the vision is expressed in the affirmation that Abraham is father of all Israel and every person is his child (Genesis 15:5). Israel has a vision of all people drawn into community around the will of God (Isaiah 2:2-4). The church in the New Testament has a parallel vision of all persons being drawn under the lordship and fellowship of Jesus (Matthew 28:16-20). In the book of Acts there is the Holy Spirit who seeks to create a single community (Acts 2:43-47).

The biblical vision for peace is that all persons are children of a single family, members of single tribe, heirs of a single hope, and bearers of a single destiny, namely, the care and management of all of God's creation. Brueggemann points out that the term used to express the meaning of this vision is *shalom*. Shalom is the biblical term used to summarize the biblical vision of peace that resists all our tendencies to division, hostility, fear, drivenness, and misery. Shalom is the substance of the biblical vision of one community embracing all creation. It is this vision of peace that the Holy Spirit seeks to keep alive in our world.

When it comes right down to it we are all for peace. The general consensus of most is: "I am for peace. I am against war." But the question is, "How?" We all know where we should be, but we disagree on the peace plan to get us there. How and in what direction is the Holy Spirit leading us in our quest for peace today?

The *Corpus Christi*, the body of Christ, is a shalom community, whose strength of community is maintained through the Holy Spirit. In the New Testament, the foundation of the body of Christ, the community of faith, is love. Love is the cement that holds the community together. Love is essential. The church is where people love one another. It is a community where people are more important than property or things, where peace is acquired through atonement rather than attainment. It is a community where swords are beaten into plowshares, and spears into pruning hooks; where iron is for tilling rather than for killing. The church is a community where the people do not "learn war any more." It is a community where the most powerful force is spiritual rather than physical.

94

The Absence Of Peace

Peace is the most sought after thing in the world. It has been the goal of governments, presidents, kings, princes, nations and the United Nations. It has been the subject of more prayers, sermons, litanies, and worship services than any other single subject. However, it remains the most elusive.

Some have become cynical in this long and, what they have considered, futile quest for peace. Thomas Hardy, the English poet, wrote after World War I,

> *Peace upon earth was said; we sing it.*
> *And pay a million priests to bring it.*
> *After two thousand years of mass.*
> *We've got as far as poison gas.*

Although Hardy was in a typical, cynical mood, yet there is a measure of truth in his words that causes us pain and shame.

The reality is that the world is cruel and peace is absent. Jeremiah cried, " 'Peace, peace,' when there is no peace" (8:11). The precarious peace we do have is preserved by a balance of terror based on the might of weaponry. What kind of peace is that? Several years ago, Thomas Edison said, "What the mind of man can create, the heart of man can control." Can we? That seems to be today's question that still needs an answer.

The movie, *Dr. Strangelove*, three decades ago reminded us that the real doomsday machine is not the bomb, but human beings themselves. The UNESCO charter of the United Nations states flatly, "Wars begin in the minds of men." The bomb is a product of selfishness and sin. War is a consequence of human sinfulness. Thomas Aquinas, centuries ago in the scholastic period of the church, reminded us that things in and of themselves are not evil. Bombs are not evil. American technology is not evil. Leonard Sweet, in his book *The Lion's Pride*, is absolutely right when he says, "Evil comes from what one does with what one has." Weapons are the tools of human intentions.

95

The Moral Dimensions Of Peace

The book of Genesis is on target. The author hit the nail right on the head when he described the four basic problems of the world that beset Adam and Eve as being sex, greed, pride, and violence. They are all fundamentally spiritual issues. Therefore, our fundamental problem is not weaponry. It is ideas, values, priorities, thinking and theology. It is within the church, the body of Christ, that the issues of world peace must be met head on. These are moral problems and they need moral answers. These are theological problems and they need theological answers. The Holy Spirit comes to lead us to the truthful and moral dimensions of peace.

Therefore, peace, freedom, liberty and justice cannot come from weaponry but divinity, not from the mind of men and women, but the heart of God, through the Holy Spirit. The church can say to the Pentagon, "You have it all wrong." National security is not in the "hands of the right force," but in the "hands of the force of right."

The most powerful, the most invincible, the strongest national defense that we can have is spiritual not material. The words of Zachariah hit home: "Not by might, nor by power, but by my spirit says the Lord." Down deep we have known this all along. It has been part of our Christian education since we were children.

Peace is a matter of will, not weaponry. Sweet asks, "If it took one stone for David to slay Goliath, why do we require millions?" The answer seems to be: The weaker we become as a nation in the realm of the spirit, the harder we try to be stronger in might. The weaker we become in will, the desire there is to become stronger in rhetoric and weapons. Sweet concludes, "If we would perspire more for peace, we would bleed less for war."

Peace Amid Conflict

Jesus talks to his disciples about the coming of the Holy Spirit and inward peace in an angry world. "Peace, I leave with you ...." What did this peace mean for Jesus? It did not mean living in the absence of violence and conflict. Jesus made this statement about peace while being in the "eye of the hurricane." His peace was being experienced amid the conspiracy of his enemies who were planning to take his life and bring about his downfall.

Jesus was quick to point out to them that the world was not able to give this kind of peace. The Roman world of Jesus' time defined peace as the absence of war and conflict. This is much the same way that we define peace in our world today. This was not the kind of peace that Jesus was talking about. His life was surrounded by boiling hostility, hatred and violence. There were those who were planning to take his life. The cross for his crucifixion was being prepared by the carpenters who were fitting the cross-member. His accusers were assembling to scheme and plan their strategy for the taking of his life. Amid these circumstances, he said to his disciples when his world was falling apart, "My legacy to you, my gift to you, is my peace." From the circumstances that were swirling about this life at this time, peace appeared to be the very thing he did not have.

When the Dow Jones is falling, unemployment appears imminent, health is declining, the diagnosis is unchanging, and danger is impending — it is then that the peace of Christ is prevailing and enduring.

The time, the day, the moment will come when peace will become the most valuable and precious possession of life. One of the most emotional scenes on television of the earthquake in San Francisco was the picture of the man standing near the collapsed Interstate 880, pleading with the officers to allow him to go in and search for his son. He pleaded, "Let me go in and look for my son. Maybe he is in a coma, maybe he is unconscious, if only I can get to him." The officers had to restrain him from going in amid the rubble because of the danger to his own life. The cameras would come back hour after hour and the man was still there waiting and pleading. It was a very heart-wrenching moment for those watching on television. What is one to do in a moment like that? Is it possible to know a sense of peace in the midst of such tumult and pain? For Jesus this peace is a peace even in the midst of hostility, even in the face of Calvary and death. He said to his disciples, ''I have this peace; this peace I give to you.''

The Holy Spirit And Inner Peace

Nowhere does the Bible teach that the righteous shall not suffer, or face adversity, or not live amid turbulent events. Religion in the Bible is not an insurance policy where one pays the premiums in offerings and attendance, thus protected and sheltered from suffering and pain. Nowhere is God represented as bribing people into God's service by rewards of prosperity or immunity from adversity. The apostle reminds us, ''We are ... fellow heirs with Christ, provided we suffer with him in order that we may also be glorified with him'' (Romans 8:17).

The Holy Spirit is a presence, a force, a power to see us through. Even for that father standing by the rubble of Highway 880, looking for his son, it is possible to say, ''On Christ the solid rock I stand, (when literally in an earthquake) all other ground is sinking sand.'' Can you picture this setting of Jesus with his disciples? They are confused, bewildered, scared, uneasy, and afraid. He said to them, ''Peace, I leave with you ... Let not your hearts be troubled, neither let them be afraid.'' How often during their lifetime the disciples would relive that experience and remember those words.

There is a fable, told by Leonard Sweet in *The Lion's Pride*, about an oriental monarch who met Pestilence on the road to Baghdad. The monarch asked, ''What are you going to do there?'' Pestilence replied, ''I am going to kill 5,000 people.'' On the way back the monarch met Pestilence again, ''You are a liar,'' he thundered. ''You killed 25,000 people.'' ''Oh, no,'' said Pestilence, ''I killed 5,000. It was fear that killed the rest.'' Fear kills! It tears life apart. It destroys faith and hope. It obscures our vision and saps our strength. We are not only afraid, but at times scared, by what is happening in us, to us, and

98

around us. The peace that Jesus gives us is that which anchors the soul in the time of storm. As the hymn writer states,

When all around my soul gives way,
He then is my rock and stay.

How discouraged God must feel when he looks at his world of creation and sees the bloodshed, violence, and destruction that men, women and nations have brought upon one another. We seem to be hell-bent on destroying the environment and ourselves with it.

Morality And Peace

Isaiah declared that "righteousness will yield peace" (Isaiah 32:17 NEB). There is a relationship between morality and peace. A relationship that we have not yet seemed to understand or comprehend. We have not aimed high enough in our desires for peace. We have allowed the politicians to convince us that the way to peace is in a state of armed preparedness. They have told us that we should set our sights on the balance of power, hoping against hope that fear would restrain the strife. In no sense could fear make possible our quest for peace. The Bible knows nothing about a peace that is based on fear, but rather a peace that is based on righteousness.

Isaiah said that the effect of righteousness is peace. Why is it that peace is so elusive in our day? First, peace is so elusive because of the unrighteousness of a deep-seated racism in our world. No city, no state, no country can have peace until it resolves the question of race. Our greatest threat is not bombs or arms, but racism. Nothing has done more in the twentieth century to kill, destroy, inflict pain or suffering than racism. This is true from the Third Reich to the apartheid of South Africa. We will never see peace in the streets of Soweto, New York or Miami until we conquer that battle and allow God's love to prevail in our lives.

For man, racism is a spiritual problem. We must, at all costs, guard against such divisive, racial attitudes in the body of Christ — the church. The fact is, such divisive and racial attitudes do exist in the church. It is incredible how such crippling racial attitudes within the church have distracted us from our primary task of being peacekeepers and reconcilers for Jesus Christ in our broken and divided world. **We need a reprise of Pentecost in order to bridge the difference of race and culture in the church today.**

The Possibility Of Peace

Regardless of what has happened or what is happening now, peace for our world is possible because the Holy Spirit is ever working for peace in our world. It is God's will for this world. The prophet Micah declared,

> *In the days to come ...*
> *God will settle disputes among the nations,*
> *among the great powers near and far.*
> *They will hammer their swords into plows*
> *and their spears into pruning knives.*
> *Nations will never again go to war,*
> *never prepare for battle again.*
> *Everyone will live in peace ....* — Micah 4:1-4 (GNB)

Peace is possible because it is the will of God and the Holy Spirit desires to bring peace.

Peace is possible because the Bible gives us the assurance that there is within this troubled world and behind the mysteries of time and space a sovereign God who is on the side of justice and on the side of peace. We shall begin to be God's instruments for righteousness and peace as our own minds and hearts are at peace with God. In God's will is our peace. Peace is an integral part of our commitment to Jesus Christ as Lord and Savior. It is the Christian's responsibility to work for peace.

100

Peace is possible if we work as hard for peace as we have for war. We have paid a high price for the waging of war. I wonder how different the history of this century may have been if we had been able to save the lives of the young men and women who were killed in its wars. The high price of war is not only paid by those who live through it, but by all the generations to come. Many of us are old enough to remember what shortages and discomforts were endured, what wealth was poured out, what terrible sufferings were borne, and what lives were lost in World War II, as well as in the Korean and Vietnam wars. What a different world this would be if we would be willing to pay at least as high a price in economic terms for peace.

Personal Peace

We cannot become the instruments of peace and reconciliation until our own hearts and minds are at peace with God. The violence in our world results from the conflict and turmoil in our own lives. The divisions in the world are the divisions within our hearts. We will not be at peace with the world until we are at peace with ourselves. The Holy Spirit brings to us what Paul describes as the fruits of the Spirit: love, joy, and peace (Galatians 5:22). The apostle goes on to declare, "If we live by the Spirit, let us walk also by the Spirit" (Galatians 5:25).

In God's peace is our peace. It begins with us. The work for peace begins with the first person we meet. Regardless whether that person is black or white, rich or poor, homeless or affluent, transient or neighbor, the peace within your soul, the peace in our world, depends on how you treat that person.

The War, Our Conscience, And Lent

(As I write this section I have just returned from an early morning Ash Wednesday service and the coalition forces are about to invade Kuwait.)

General Patton, the most flamboyant and aggressive of American generals in World War II, was able on occasion to reflect on the ultimate paradox of war. One such incident was when he wrote in his journal at the time of the allied invasion of France, "An arresting sight in one French village were the crucifixes located on the top of long poles at each corner of the intersection. They were used by the signal corps as supplementary telephone poles. I could not help but think of the incongruity between the crosses and the lethal messages that passed over the wires."

In war we always make some appeal to moral idealism. We have regarded war as something of a tragic necessity, justified if fought with conscientious instincts to repel an intolerable wrong. Such reasoning has produced the classic doctrine of the "just war." Most people in most wars think of their own cause as justifiable. To gain support for war, religion and nationalism are forced into a formidable alliance. Without thinking of the incongruity, Christian theology and symbolism, like those crucifixes in that French village, are used to support a lethal message. The President has sought, and for the most part received, the support of the churches for the war effort in the Persian Gulf.

For the last several weeks our minds have been full of such words as killing fields, smart bombs, precision bombing, sorties, collateral damage, KIA's, EPW's, and POW's. This morning I attended an early Ash Wednesday service in our chapel and received communion. I was reminded of the broken body of Christ and I found myself thinking upon the Prince of Peace, the Suffering Servant, who has asked us to love our enemies, pray for those who would despitefully use us, to forgive seventy times seven and to resist evil.

The Christ, who is the focus of our attention during our Lenten pilgrimage, was a nonviolent man, who refused to take the sword, and told us that a man has no greater love than to lay down his life for his friend. This morning as I prayed at the altar I was conscious of a life and teachings that were far different from all that I have been hearing for the past several months.

The life of Jesus and his teachings throw a mighty question mark against the warlike ways of men and women. If we don't know what to do with them, we cannot easily forget them. During this service I asked myself, "Is it possible that we are practicing violence in the pursuit of goals that are attainable only by violence?" We should not set limits on the possibilities of nonviolence, or on the potential power in Christlike living, when we have given it such little chance.

The sayings of Jesus are parabolic, situational, metaphorical, and dramatic. They should disturb us, awaken us to new styles of human awareness, shatter rigid preconceptions, and lure us with unrealized possibilities for peace and justice.

This morning the words of that outstanding hymn by Harry Emerson Fosdick came to mind:

> *Cure thy children's warring madness,*
> *Bend our pride to thy control;*
> *Shame our wanton, selfish gladness,*
> *Rich in things, poor in soul.*
> *Grant us wisdom, grant us courage,*
> *Lest we miss thy kingdom's goal.*

For Further Reflection And Study

1. Define the biblical meaning of *shalom.*

2. How and in what direction is the Holy Spirit leading us in our quest for peace today?

3. Comment on Leonard Sweet's comment, "Evil comes from what one does with what one has. Weapons are the tools of human intentions."

4. Do you agree that our fundamental problems are moral problems, that need moral answers?

5. What is the relationship between morality and peace?

6. What are the possibilities for peace? What role does the Holy Spirit seek to play in world peace?

7. What is the relationship between the Holy Spirit and non-violence?

8. How diligently do you think the Christian Church is working toward world peace with justice? Is the church part of the solution or the problem?

Chapter Ten

The Spirit-filled Life

The promise is that the Holy Spirit would lead us into new things. These new things would involve new discoveries, new knowledge and understanding of God and ourselves. The fact is we become so accustomed to the old ways of doing things that we are not so sure we want the Holy Spirit to challenge us with such newness.

The Challenge Of New Things

This is the problem that Jesus faced. He was well aware that he came with new ideas for a new way of life, containing new concepts of truth. The power of his teachings had the radicalness of a new birth. It was like being born all over again. Jesus knew that he was going to have a difficult time. So he shared with his audience this simple parable because he knew of their temptation to keep the old ways of thinking and doing. He told them about the wine and the wineskins. Not having bottles in those days the wine was stored in animal skins. Since the new wine was giving off gases and expanding it was placed in new wineskins, because they were supple, soft and elastic, capable of expanding with the pressure. Jesus said it would never be advisable to put the new wine into old wineskins, because they are dry, brittle, and with no elasticity. Since they could not expand with the pressure, they would eventually crack open and the wine would be lost.

To put this into contemporary terms, our minds must be elastic enough to receive and contain new ideas. It seems that we must always struggle against the prejudice of a shut mind. The coming of the Holy Spirit would bring change and change is not something that the church easily accepts. When new life in the Spirit comes upon the church old ways, manners, words, phrases, creeds, and theology seem to come apart and crack — like old wineskins. Why is there such rigidity against new life in the Spirit? One reason may be that such newness would bring about a change in behavior. The old becomes familiar whereas the new brings new demands and possibly sacrifices. Behavior is not easily changed without a struggle. This newness is expressed clearly by the apostle in 2 Corinthians 5:17, "If anyone is in Christ, there is a new creation: everything old is passed away; see, everything has become new" (NRSV).

Giving Up Old Ways

It is hard for us to give up the old wineskins. We pour the activities of the spirit-filled modern Christians into old forms of behavior that were never meant for them. We pour the truth of Christian teachings into worn-out and archaic words and language that no one understands. We pour our newfound joy in the Holy Spirit into old, formal, stuffy, expressionless forms of worship that excite no one. It would be a pity that we would hold to old forms, allowing the wine of new truth to be spilt. The new wine of new life in the Spirit ought not be poured into the legalism of the past.

The new must be allowed to have its own integrity. Jesus' new way of life demands new forms of expression. The new wine of the Spirit breaks through the rigid forms of the legalism of the past. George Buttrick declared that "there is a red-tide running from the winepress of Calvary that cannot be easily restrained" (*The Parables of Jesus,* p. 8).

The Fruits Of The Spirit

When we think about the spirit-filled life we think about the list of the fruits of the Spirit in Galatians 5. Here the apostle is contrasting life with and without the Spirit. In verse 19 he describes in very vivid terms the works of the flesh, listing

106

such things as: licentiousness, jealousy, anger, strife, and envy, concluding that such things are not the fruits of the Spirit. Beginning with verse 22, he lists the fruits of the Spirit beginning with love and adding joy, peace, patience, kindness, generosity, faithfulness, gentleness, and self-control, declaring that there is no law against such things.

Note, that when the apostle talks about the works of the flesh, for the word "works" he used the Greek word *erga*, the plural. When he talks about the "fruit" of the Spirit, he uses *carpos,* the singular. He describes the works (plural) of the flesh in contrast to the fruit (singular) of the Spirit. This distinction grew out of his experience. Before his life in the Spirit his life was in rebellion against God. At that time he was at cross purposes, splitting and fragmenting his life. He hints of this in Romans 6:19, when he says that the good that he wants to do, he cannot do. Then the Spirit entered his life, integrating his life with God and others. The Spirit centered his life in the unifying love of Christ.

The apostle uses the singular, "the fruit of the Spirit," because there is one fruit, that being love. The central, integrating factor of the Spirit is love, the love of God through Christ. All the rest are merely the results of love: joy, peace, patience, kindness, generosity, faithfulness, gentleness and self-control. The apostle says the same thing about the gifts of the Spirit in 1 Corinthians 12: teaching, faith, healing, knowledge, prophecy and the speaking in tongues. Then in 1 Corinthians 13, he declares that the greatest gift of all is love. He said if a person had many outstanding gifts, but if he did not have love, the other gifts did not mean very much.

The works of the flesh: licentiousness, jealousy, selfishness, and strife act like a centrifugal force that seeks to tear life apart. They move life away from having a center and a wholeness. Therapists will tell you they are the factors that cause life to disintegrate. Whereas, love in the Spirit is the centripetal force that pulls life together. This love is also multidirectional in that it is a love toward self, for now in the Spirit you feel good about yourself. It is a love toward others who are no longer a threat or a fear, but are a support bringing to life a sense of fulfillment. It is, above all, a love toward God which brings everything together causing life to have a center and a wholeness.

New Power

It is a good thing that we are aware of our shortcomings as a church and as individuals. But it would be disastrous if we become paralyzed through discouragement. It is in human weakness that the power of the Holy Spirit is made manifest. This is the message of Pentecost. We are promised power, at every point where the need is most evident. Pentecost was a day that the apostle could never forget. Through the Holy Spirit Christ would be forever a living presence in the world. The Spirit saturated the apostle's preaching, writing, and behavior. Neither can we ever afford to forget that event or ever permit it to slip from our memory, our message or our lives. We must remember that on that Day of Pentecost every man and woman heard the apostle's message in his own language. Whatever else that means, William Barclay points out that "the disciples were empowered by the Spirit to speak the message of the gospel in such a way that it found a road straight to the heart of men and women of every origin and of every background" (*Expository Times,* May 1982, p. 245). The secret seemed to be that the message was actualized in the apostles' experience before it was formulated in their speech. If we should ever lose the Pentecost experience from our life together, we would have lost heart, soul, spirit, and vitality from our Christian experience. To lose the Spirit from our lives would be like owning a modern, powerful, expensive automobile with no access to fuel. Things would look good but you would not be able to go anywhere because of the lack of power. Not only do automobiles stand still because of the lack of a power source, but so do human lives.

You may still feel that Pentecost was a rather strange and bizarre moment with the rush of a mighty wind, the appearing of tongues of fire, speaking in a new, unifying language of love and reconciliation, with unusual forms of religious enthusiasm to the point that the apostles were mistaken for people intoxicated by a new wine. Being the rationalists we are, we look somewhat skeptically upon it all, but I would imagine that the present day emptiness, dryness, dullness, and superficiality of modern Christianity would have astonished first century Christians. The church prospers or declines in its fortunes in proportion to its belief in and experience of the Holy Spirit. There were patterns of Pentecost that should be patterns for us. These patterns are essential to us if we are going to maintain a spirit-filled life.

Spirit-filled Worship

One of the patterns of Pentecost that is essential for us to maintain is a spirit-filled worship service. Before we engage in mission, evangelism, education, or stewardship we first must experience God in worship. In spirit-filled worship we encounter the presence of God. Worship is the center and the hub of congregational life together. Worship is the most important, central factor in the life of a congregation. If it doesn't happen in worship it will probably never happen. A cold, lifeless, spiritless church most certainly has a cold, lifeless, and spiritless worship service. Leonard Sweet, in talking about the worship service, states that "the New Testament knows no other kind of church but a pentecostal church, no other kind of believer but a charismatic believer." The gospel may be preached and the sacraments administered, but unless personal gifts and graces are articulated, activated, and celebrated, "our efforts yield little more than hallowing of hollowness at worst or ho-hum spirits at best" (*New Life in the Spirit,* p. 45).

Why is our evangelism so weak and anemic? Could it be the lack of the Spirit's presence in our worship? How can we share what we do not have? How can we tell others what we have not experienced ourselves? God must first speak to us before we ever speak God's word to someone else. Isaiah's experience of worship was so real, awesome, and so cleansing that when the Lord asked, "Who will go for me?" Isaiah responded, "Here am I. Send me." The immediate results of this spirit-filled worship made Isaiah the willing instrument and vessel of God's prophetic word to others.

Being A Witness

Another pattern of Pentecost essential for spirit-filled life is witness. When the apostles were given the promise of the Holy Spirit in Acts 1:8 they were to be witnesses in Judea and Samaria and to the ends of the earth. Peter's first response to this experience of Pentecost was to witness. He was on his feet facing the crowd. Gone was his self-consciousness about his previous denial and failure. Gone was his feeling of inadequacy, timidity, reluctance and his old fear of people. He spoke boldly out of a new awareness of God's forgiveness, cleansing, and empowerment. His awfulness had encountered God's awesomeness. Here he was on his feet facing a huge throng and the words of his first sermon just seemed to flow. It may not have been an object lesson in homiletics and possibly Fred Craddock may not have given him a passing grade in structure, but you could not fault his delivery and the results it produced. If response would be any measure of success then this sermon was magnificent, possibly the most successful sermon in the entire New Testament.

Peter gave a model of what all witnessing ought to be. He had a simple, direct message that all understood. He spoke directly to the needs of the people. He called for a decision on the part of his listeners. Look at Acts 2:38.

> *Repent, and be baptized every one of you in the name of Jesus Christ so that your sins may be forgiven; and you will receive the gift of the Holy Spirit.*
> — Acts 2:38 NRSV

The onlookers at the Day of Pentecost accused the disciples of being filled with new wine, in other words, being

110

drunk. Peter observed that they were confusing inebriation with inspiration so he declared, "Men of Judea and all who live in Jerusalem, let this be known to you, and listen to what I say. Indeed, these are not drunk, as you suppose, ... this is what was spoken through the prophet Joel" (Acts 2:14b-16 NRSV).

New Wine

The association of wine with the Spirit is an interesting one. Those who accused the apostles of being drunk were making fun, mocking them, but they were not that far from the truth. A person who is drunk with new wine usually experiences three things. He sees things he never saw before. He says things he never said before. He does things he never did before.

After being filled with the new wine of the Spirit the apostles did see things they had never seen before. When the Spirit enters one's life eyes are opened to see things in a different light and things take on new meaning. This is what Jesus promised in John 16:13, "When the Spirit of truth comes, he will guide you into all the truth ..."

A person filled with new wine will say things he or she never said before. This is probably the most obvious characteristic of the inebriated person — wine loosens the tongue. So does the Holy Spirit. This was the most startling aspect of the day of Pentecost, "All of them were filled with the Holy Spirit and began to speak in other languages, as the Spirit gave them ability" (Acts 2:4 NRSV). The Holy Spirit loosens our tongues to speak in the language of the Spirit.

A person filled with new wine will attempt things he never did before. He will become bold and reckless. A person filled with the Holy Spirit will also attempt new things in a rather bold manner bordering on recklessness, to the point that onlookers would view it as a drunken act of foolishness. The Holy Spirit produces the unpredictable in human life, ever full of surprises, using the most unlikely person as spokesperson. The Spirit never does things the way we expect or think they should

111

be done. If you look closely at the biblical narrative you will discover that is the way God always brings about his purpose.

Even from the beginning, things appeared a bit reckless. Abraham was called by God and God promised to make him the father of a great nation that would be as numerous as the sands of the sea and the stars of the sky. It all started with a man who had his AARP card and had been receiving senior citizen discounts for nearly 40 years. His wife Sarah, in the words of Frederick Buechner, had one foot in the grave and the other in the maternity ward. No wonder she laughed when God told her what he was about to do with her life. From the beginning God has been unpredictable and so are God's people who are led by the Spirit, whose actions sometimes border on the reckless and foolish.

Come to think of it, it will always seem foolish to the world to deny yourself and take up a cross; to love an enemy; to take one of your two coats and give it away; to bless those who curse and mistreat you; to be a good Samaritan and stop to minister to an injured traveler on the dangerous Jericho road. But those filled with the Spirit will do those things, regardless of how foolish it makes them look.

Back To Basics

In Search of Excellence is a book that became an overnight national bestseller in the secular marketplace. Its popularity was due, in part, to the fact that it is not a theoretical volume based on untried ideas and academic dreams. The authors, Tom Peters and Bob Waterman, told about what their research uncovered regarding the best-run companies in the U.S.

Business men and women all over the country have appreciated their work because in plain, everyday language they relate how companies can be successful in the complicated marketplace of conglomerates and other complex business circumstances. Their conclusion was,

The excellent companies were, above all, brilliant on the basics. Tools did not substitute for thinking. Intellect didn't overpower wisdom. Analysis didn't impede action. Rather, these companies worked hard to keep things simple in a complex world.

There are two important words that stand out in this statement: simple and complex. The most successful companies were "brilliant on the basics" and "simple in the complex world."

People want basic answers and simple solutions, not simplistic solutions, but solutions that they can understand and are easy to comprehend. People want answers that they can grasp and understand in their search for excellence in their own lives, especially at a time when life appears so circuitous, muddled and perplexing. New life in the Spirit seeks to get us back to the basics. When the apostle talks about the fruit of the Spirit he is talking about a language that we can understand. Nothing could be more basic when he tells us that the life in the Spirit is one of love, joy, peace, kindness, faithfulness, and goodness. That kind of basic language we can understand.

Life In The Spirit

E. Stanley Jones, Methodist missionary to India tells the story in his book *Growing Spirituality* about a fictional person who lived out a fantasy life. All this person had to do was think something and poof! — it happened. He imagines a house and poof — there it is: 15 bedrooms, three stories and servants to wait on his every need. In a place like that he needs a fine car — poof! He has the world's finest cars: Jaguar, Rolls and Mercedes, complete with chauffeurs or he can drive them himself. Having no other place to travel he comes home and wishes for a sumptuous meal — poof! There before him is mouth-watering, exquisite food and he eats alone. Being bored and realizing he is not really enjoying all of this, he whispers to one of his attendants, "I'd rather be in hell than here." To which the attendant replies, "Where do you think you are?"

An empty, lonely, isolated, spiritless existence is the worst existence of all.

A life without the Spirit creates an itch for things and a lust for more. It is a virus draining our souls of happy contentment. In a life without the Spirit a man never earns enough, a woman is never beautiful enough, clothes are never fashionable enough, gadgets are not modern enough, houses are never big enough, food is never fancy enough, relationships are never romantic enough, and life is never full enough. It puts you in a mad race that you can never win. Satisfaction comes when we step off the escalator of desire and say,

> *Come, Holy Spirit my soul inspire,*
> *Ignite within me a celestial fire.*

For Further Reflection And Study

1. In what way is the Holy Spirit leading us into new things? Why is it hard to give up old ways?

2. Why is there such rigidity against new life in the Spirit?

3. Comment on the statement that "the church prospers or declines in its fortunes in proportion to its belief and experience of the Holy Spirit."

4. How does the Spirit impact our lives in regard to:

    a. public worship

    b. evangelism

    c. witness?

5. If the Holy Spirit seeks to bring us back to the basics of Christian living — what are the basics?

6. Describe the fruits of the spirit as defined in Galatians 5:22. How are they related to us today?

Chapter Eleven

What About The Trinity?

In our study of the Holy Spirit it is essential that serious thought be given to the Trinity. The first Christians were converts from Judaism. They were born and raised in a Jewish environment and until the Christian church was able to establish its own identity by the middle of the second century, it was considered a sect of Judaism.

The belief in one God (monotheism) was basic to Judaism and is mentioned often throughout the Old Testament. God is not a plurality, nor is God one among others. God is single and unique. The *Shema*, which became the confession of faith for the Israelite community, is expressed in Deuteronomy 6:4, "Hear, O Israel: The Lord our God is one Lord." Here there is no hint of tritheism. The Old Testament scriptures affirmed again and again that the Lord *(Yahweh)* is the only and unique God, who has been revealed in human history. In contrast to the polytheism of their neighbors, Israel declared, "The Lord is God; there is no other besides him" (Deuteronomy 4:35). There are numerous passages in Isaiah where God is declared to be unmatched in wisdom, majesty, and power. Yahweh is the creator and the Lord of all human history (See Isaiah 41:28-29; 42:17; 43:10-11; 44:7-8; 45:5-6; 46:1-2, 8-11).

Some feel there is a reference to the Trinity by the Old Testament in the frequent use of the phrase "Spirit of God" and by the use of the plural in Genesis 1:26 and 11:7 as well as the plural form of the name and nature of the divine appearance to Abraham in Genesis 18. However, there is no substantial reference to any idea of the Trinity in the Old Testament.

The Trinity In The New Testament

The early Christians took from Judiasm its sacred writings of the Old Testament accepting them as holy scripture. The Christian community accepted the understanding of God as one who stands alone as the Creator of the world, who excludes all other gods, and is yet a personal God who enters into human relationships. While there is no dogmatic statement regarding the Trinity in the New Testament there are clear references to the Godhead. In Matthew 28:19 is the great commission: "Go therefore and make disciples of all nations, baptizing them in the name of the Father and of the Son and of the Holy Spirit."

Although the church accepted from Judaism the monotheistic belief in one God, it also declared its belief in the reality of God as seen in Jesus Christ and the work of the Holy Spirit. The New Testament reveals a growing realization of a unique relationship between God, Jesus Christ and the Holy Spirit. How these three are related was to become a source of discussion and debate for centuries.

Although we must remember that the term "the Trinity" is not a biblical term yet Donald McKim in his book, *Theological Turning Points* (p. 6ff), reminds us that the actions of God, Jesus Christ and the Holy Spirit are the themes of the New Testament. There is no doubt that in the Synoptic Gospels there is a clear affirmation of the oneness of God. However, within the Synoptics, God's unique relationship to Jesus is expressed in such titles as *Lord, Son of Man, Son of God,* the *only begotten of the Father,* and the *holy One of God.* While in the writings of John, God is the *Word* (logos — see John 1) and the *Son of God* (John 3:16, 20:31), and *God the Father* is frequently used in John 1:14, 10:38, 14:6.

There is a strong implication in the Gospels that the Holy Spirit is a person. This is particularly true in Acts where the Spirit is said *to speak* (1:16, 8:29), *to send* (13:4), *to bear witness* (5:32), *to prevent* (16:7), and *to appoint* (20:28). In Paul's writings the Holy Spirit is more fully active in the ordinary

118

life of the Christian. Paul points to the personality of the Holy Spirit in Romans 8:14, 16; Galatians 4:6; Ephesians 4:30; 1 Corinthians 2:11.

McKim points to a number of New Testament passages that show what he calls a triadic or Trinitarian pattern *(Theological Turning Points*, p. 7f). Such a pattern occurs in God's announcement to Mary through the angel's words, "The Holy Spirit will come upon you, and the power of the Most High will overshadow you; therefore the child to be born will be called holy, the Son of God" (Luke 1:35). Likewise, in Luke's account of Jesus' baptism, God is portrayed as speaking in conjunction with the Holy Spirit. All three persons are mentioned in the baptism of Jesus in Matthew 28:19. In the opening section of Acts (1:1-6), the Father, Jesus and the Holy Spirit are mentioned together. Further evidence of such a triadic or trinitarian pattern can be found in Acts 2:33, 38-39; 9:17-20; 10:30.

In the writings of the apostle Paul the triadic formula frequently occurs as seen in 2 Corinthians 13:14. The oneness of the Father, Son and Spirit is seen in Ephesians 4:4-6. Paul expresses this oneness in the work of redemption: God sent Christ, who was crucified, was raised, and ascended, so "that we might receive the promise of the Spirit through faith" (Galatians 3:14).

There is clear evidence in the New Testament that the Holy Spirit is portrayed as a divine force and power who possesses a distinct personal existence. When the early church was asked, "Who is God?" they sought to answer the question on the basis of the Old and New Testaments. Therefore, they answered in light of such scriptural evidence that while God is Father, Son, and Holy Spirit, somehow God is also one God. McKim admits that such a confession needed a much fuller elaboration and this was to become the task of Christian theologians for the next several centuries *(ibid.* p. 8). I would add that this is still the task of theology today.

The Trinity In The Early Church

It is evident that the early church seriously wrestled with the question of the Trinity during the first three centuries. It is crucial for us as we continue to discuss the nature of God's identity that we formulate our response on the basis of biblical teaching and in thought forms that can be understood and communicated. Let us keep this in mind as we continue our study.

A definition or the explanation of the Trinity has always been difficult for the Christian Church. Rudolph Otto in his book, *The Idea of the Holy*, claims that the basis for all religious experience is the sense of something mysterious, fascinating and awesome. It involves a sense of a presence or a power that we cannot clearly identify or pin down. It leads to the notion of a God who is always present, always likely to be encountered, and yet also a God who is illusive.

Otto goes on to say that a God who would be explained by the human mind or reason would cease to exist. In approaching the concept of the Trinity which involves mystery and for many ambiguity, we need to pursue such study and inquiry by asking ourselves, "How does the Trinity take on meaning in expressing the reality of God?" In other words what kind of meaning does the Trinity have when it is expressed in relation to Christian experience?

When discussing the Trinity, Christians often fall into a kind of tritheism. They tend to think of Father, Son, and Spirit as three kings trying to sit on the same throne, or of a divine committee of three. It is so easy to lapse into tritheism that church members cannot be blamed for doing so.

When tritheism prevails in religion, the Father and the Son get most of the attention. We associate the Father with creation, providence, and the last judgment. The Son is related to atonement and the church. Whereas, the Holy Spirit is relegated to third place and is restricted to applying or reproducing the actions of the Son in the primary area of ecclesiastical and personal life.

120

Colin Morris, in his book *The Word and Words*, declares that Trinity Sunday is the preacher's Waterloo. He said if the preacher is prudent he will go down with a strategic bout of the flu on Saturday preventing him from entering the pulpit on Trinity Sunday. I don't think Morris needs to worry about this because most preachers never even think about the Trinity on Trinity Sunday. He is convinced that the doctrine of Trinity is probably the most conclusive example of the futility of trying to rationalize a mystery — to imprison God in a web of words, to pin him down like a specimen butterfly in a showcase. But what basic Christian doctrine does not have a mystery? Did not the apostle declare, "Lo, I tell you a mystery" (1 Corinthians 15:51a)?

The Trinity And Religious Experience

But the purpose of Christian doctrine is not to attempt to rationalize or solve a mystery, but to explain an experience. All the metaphors used to describe Christ's saving work are attempts to describe the sense of deliverance in the experience of the first Christians. The theories of atonement are not expositions of the mechanics of salvation, but the expression of salvation. It would appear that the experience of salvation in Christ gave birth to the doctrine of the Trinity. The prevailing thought has been that of a God whose name and nature is love, being revealed himself in the person of Christ and eternally available to all through the Spirit. We seek to understand it, but first we need to make sure we experience it.

One of our problems in regard to the doctrine of the Trinity is that we do things backwards. We start with formulas, creeds, and the explanation of doctrine — therefore they appear as dull and not making much sense to us. The early Christian did not begin with creeds or explanations, but with experience. Creeds and doctrines have meaning to us as God becomes real to us in our human experience. It would appear that the doctrine of the Trinity takes on meaning as a way of expressing the reality of God. Therefore, personal religious experience precedes creed and doctrines.

In our attempt to understand this mystery, we must begin by realizing that the doctrine of the Trinity is not a bit of speculation dreamed up by the theologians. It grew out of an attempt by early Christians to interpret and make sense of their experience of God. It signifies that within one essence of the Godhead we have tried to distinguish three "persons" who are neither three gods on the one side, nor three parts or modes of God on the other, but coequally and coeternally God.

Theologians are careful to point out that when attention to the Trinity declines distortions of the Christian understanding of God appear. The Trinity expresses the distinctively Christian understanding of God. If this understanding of God declines, then the church is in danger of losing its identity. Migliore is wise to point out that in the Christian church the experience of the Holy Spirit is either the experience of the Spirit of the triune God or it is a divisive and ever destructive experience. Our United Methodist Church in Florida yearly has a conference on the Holy Spirit. I have refrained from attending until it is preceded by a conference on God the Father and Christ the Son.

The Trinity And The Christian Life

Today as we try to understand the mystery of the Trinity, we must first realize that the doctrine of the Trinity is not an idea created from the minds of the church theologians. Also, it is the only festival of the Christian Year that is not associated with an event but with a doctrine. For this reason, some feel that the doctrine of the Trinity is irrelevant and is not really related to the concerns of life. Why has this doctrine persisted over the centuries? Why is it still paramount in Christian devotion? On Sundays we still sing, "Glory be to the Father, and to the Son, and to the Holy Spirit." We continue to use the Doxology which ends, "Praise to the Father, Son and Holy Spirit." One of our most popular hymns happens to be, "Holy, holy, holy, Lord God Almighty ... God in three Persons, blessed Trinity." Our babies are still baptized and our young people married, "In the name of the Father and of the Son and of the Holy Spirit." Our worship still closes with the Apostle's threefold blessing.

Why is the doctrine so persistent? Because the doctrine of the Trinity is the Christian way of summing up what we believe about life. What it says is that life is shaped around three central realities: "The *grace* of our Lord Jesus Christ and the *love* of God and the *fellowship* of the Holy Spirit be with you all" (2 Corinthians 13:14). If we are to know God in God's fullness we must know God as the apostle Paul knew God — through the grace of our Lord Jesus Christ, through the love of God the Father, and through the communion, or fellowship, of the Holy Spirit. All three words, Father, Son and Holy Spirit, are of course, metaphors, words which tell of experiences which only images can convey. God is not a separate being; God is being itself. God is the life and power and love which is revealed to us in the life and death and resurrection of Jesus Christ, which is like a curtain opening suddenly onto an unexpected and breathtaking view. The Spirit is not a separate being, but God is, indistinguishable from our own human experience, and awakening us to all that is good and lovely and true within that experience.

The Trinity Affirms The Reality Of God

In essence, our use of the Trinity is our way of expressing how we have experienced God. The Trinity can be part of our affirmation of the Christian faith. It affirms for us the reality of God. Every Sunday when we recite the Apostles' Creed we are declaring our belief in the Trinity. We are affirming belief in "God the Father Almighty, maker of heaven and earth." The One who creates, directs, and loves it. Regardless of what happens, it is still God's world. We affirm "Jesus Christ, his only Son our Lord." Christians have been saying for centuries, if you want to know what God is like, look at Jesus. You won't see everything there is to know about God, for God is too vast and mysterious for that. But you will see what you most need to know. You will see that God is love. This mysterious transcendent God is known in Jesus Christ. Also within the creed we affirm our belief in the Holy Spirit. It is the Spirit, that powerful, creative force within us, who awakens us to life and hope. It is the Spirit who awakens us to a new awareness, appreciation, and creativity.

The Trinity is not a riddle to puzzle our minds nor is it a bit of archaic theological thinking. It is not an outdated, irrelevant dogma. Rather it is an expression of Christian experience. It is not a portrait of God, but a description of the fullness of God as we experience God. In our experience we have known God in creation as Father, in God's incarnation as Son, and in God's living presence among us as Holy Spirit. Our experience of God has been that of God above us, God among us, and God within us. Therefore, we are talking about one God, not three, but we cannot begin to say all that ought to be said about God until we describe these three ways of being. The Trinity is the Christian way of summing up what we believe about life.

Let me share with you a helpful analogy that I came across from a book written by a minister whose father was a great minister. He said, "I knew my father first as a man who lived with me, played with me, taught me and loved me." He goes on to say, "As I grew up I understood that my father was more than just my father. He had a wider work to do than just take care of me. Then came the day when I left home and went away to college. My father could not accompany me in the flesh, but I did find that he was with me in spirit. His will and his love were very much with me." He said, "I am talking about just one man, not three." But he said, "I could not possibly say all that ought to be said about my father, until I describe these three ways of being himself" (A.L. Griffith, *Expository Times,* May, 1972, p. 239). The Christian church has affirmed the doctrine of Trinity through the centuries because it describes the fullness of God as Christians have experienced God; first, in creation as Father; second, in the incarnation as Son; and third, in the living presence of the Holy Spirit.

The Christian Faith As Trinitarian Experience

Creeds become meaningful to us only as God becomes real to us in our human experience. Christianity is not a matter of accepting and believing the impossible facts or difficult explanations. Rather it is a relationship to God, and it is only as we enter into those relationships that we find doctrine helpful in explaining our relationships.

Christian truth is not abstract — it is personal. Therefore, the Trinity takes on meaning for us out of experience. When we become aware that God is the creator and we begin to live responsibly to God, then we enter into a relationship with God as a person. It is our accepting of the forgiveness of Jesus and our acknowledgement of him as the risen and living Lord of our lives, that we enter into a relationship with him as a person. It is only when we yield our lives to the direction of the Holy Spirit and enter into a relationship with the Spirit that the Spirit becomes to us a person.

The experience of the Christian faith is a trinitarian experience. It is an experience of the *grace* of our Lord Jesus Christ and the *love* of God and the *fellowship* of the Holy Spirit, bearing witness to the meaning of the Trinity.

For Further Reflection And Study

1. Describe monotheism.

2. What biblical evidence is there for the Trinity in the Old and New Testaments?

3. Define the following:

   a. tritheism

   b. triune

   c. trinity.

4. What is meant by the statement, "The doctrine of the Trinity takes on meaning for us as God becomes real in our human experiences?"

5. How does the Trinity affirm the reality of God?

6. What is meant by the statement, "The experience of the Christian faith is a trinitarian experience"?

7. Comment on Daniel Migliore's statement that "in the Christian church the experience of the Holy Spirit is either the experience of the Spirit of the triune God, or it is a divisive or even destructive experience."

Chapter Twelve

Where Is The Holy Spirit Today?

Where is the Holy Spirit in today's world? What are the characteristics of the Spirit's activity? Are there certain criteria given to us by the Christian community or the Scriptures that can be used as a yardstick to measure or test what appears to be the Spirit's activity? How can we discern the Spirit, to see if the Spirit is of God? From the earliest days of the New Testament this has been the responsibility of the church — the body of Christ. As history reveals, the church has made some good, as well as, some very poor decisions. I am convinced that such discernment is mandated by the scriptures. Discernment is a responsibility that is inescapable for the church in every age.

God Is Full Of Surprises

In seeking the whereabouts of the Holy Spirit's activity in today's world it could be that we are looking in the wrong places with false expectations. The biblical narrative reveals to us a God who is full of surprises. God through his Spirit is revealed in the most unexpected ways and manners. For one thing, when God comes to us God does not overwhelm us. God always appears to be less than God really is, rather low key, almost casual. God shuns the spectacular and prefers the ordinary. This is difficult for us to understand. We have seen too many Cecil B. DeMille films. It is hard for us to realize that the show under the big top does not matter the most or last the longest. However, all saving ideas are born small. How true this is from a biblical point of view. The two great moments of God's coming in the biblical narrative were the Exodus from Egypt and the birth of Jesus in Bethlehem. (See my two articles in the *Christian Century,* 12-2-81, p. 1245; 12-11-85, p. 1141).

God's self-disclosure in Egypt and Bethlehem reveals a loving God whose main activity is deliverance. From the bondage of Egypt was heard the cry, "Let my people go" — the words that the God of the Bible unceasingly directs against every aggression or system that threatens to enslave or impoverish.

God Chooses The Least And Lowest

God chose Israel not because it was a great nation but because it was the "least of all peoples." A tiny, insignificant nation, the doormat of the ancient world on which the great empires wiped their feet. When weak Israel was pitted against Egypt, God did not side with Pharaoh, the powerful political leader, but with the oppressed menial servants, the scum of society, the slaves. What does that say to us about the whereabouts of the Holy Spirit in today's world? God chooses common people and places to be his instruments.

This same theme is evident in the birth of Jesus. Listen to the words of Mary as she sings the *Magnificat,* her song of praise to God:

> *He has shown strength with his arm; he has scattered the proud in the thoughts of their hearts. He has brought down the powerful from their thrones, and lifted up the lowly; he has filled the hungry with good things, and sent the rich away empty.* — Luke 1:51-53 NRSV

What could be more ordinary than the birth of a child? Every time God seeks to change the course of history he allows a baby to be born — one in the bulrushes and another in a stable-cave. Who would ever have thought that such a child born in poverty and obscurity amid the Judean hills would become the highest revelation of God's love to the world? This biblical story of deliverance does help us to locate the presence of the Holy Spirit in today's world. It reveals to us that the abiding forces that direct and dominate the future are germinative — often diminutive or inconspicuous, like a mustard seed. Jesus' contemporaries found his coming so commonplace — "Is not this the carpenter, the son of Mary and the brother of James . . . are not his sisters here with us?" (Mark 6:3). They found Jesus to be rather ordinary. So much so, that they overlooked him. Familiarity puts a glaze over our eyes.

What could be more characteristic of God's coming in lowliness and meekness than Jesus' entrance into Jerusalem? He enters the city on a lowly donkey, with no spoils of victory, no gleaming armor, no gallant white stallion. His followers have no swords, but palm branches, symbols of peace. He enters the city among the shouts of children — powerless, innocent children. God comes to us like a man riding bareback on a donkey, his heels grabbing the belly of the animal to keep from falling off. God comes to us on our level, so to lift us to God's level. In the words of the apostle, Jesus became what we are that we might become what he is.

The Unexpected

We expect God to be revealed in the familiar music of the church, and for some the Spirit may come that way. For others God may come in primitive sounds that do not even resemble music. We may expect God to come in the familiar language of the Bible, especially our favorite translation. It may be possible that the Spirit may come in some strange new tongue that we find offensive and vulgar. (Remember what happened on the day of Pentecost.) Jerome's translation of the Scriptures from the Greek to the Latin in 384 A.D. was called the *Vulgate* for that very reason: the people thought Latin a vulgar language, and it was hard for them to believe that something so sacred and mysterious could be transmitted in words that were so common and ordinary.

We live in a world where power matters the most — institutional, military, financial and political power. Our world is one of ICBM's, Patriot missiles, smart bombs, space shuttles, megaton nuclear bombs and Polaris submarines. In such a world of power, what place is there for an itinerant preacher who laid down his life for others and declared that the greatest of all is the servant of all? We have difficulty in comprehending God's coming among us in such ordinary, humble terms.

The answers to our questions come directly and forthrightly, from the apostle Paul, reminding us of the true meaning of power:

> *But God chose what is foolish in the world to shame the wise; God chose what is weak in the world to shame the strong; God chose what is low and despised in the world, things that are not, to reduce to nothing things that are, so that no one might boast in the presence of God . . . . Let the one who boasts, boast in the Lord.*
> — 1 Corinthians 1:27-29, 31 NRSV

Walls Coming Down

Look at the world around us. The walls are coming down. Could this be the work of the Spirit? Is God at work in the tumbling of the Berlin Wall as he was in the tumbling of the walls of Jericho? Robert Frost in his poem, "Mending Walls," states,

> *Something there is that doesn't love a wall.*
> *That wants it down.*

The Holy Spirit does not want walls erected between people and communities. The Spirit wants them down. There is a strong temptation to declare that the mood for freedom and reform that has swept through Berlin, Prague, Leipzig, Bucharest, Russia and to some degree in both South Africa and South and Central America is the work of the Holy Spirit. We all rejoice over the prospects of freedom and democracy for Haiti.

130

One of the most hopeful signs in this movement for freedom in eastern Europe is how the church which was to some degree responsible for the walls in the first place, is now a very important part of the freedom movement in bringing the walls down. The church in Poland was the stable that gave birth to Solidarity. For Lech Walesa, it was his Christian faith that gave him the vision and the courage to bring about reform. He was joined by the church leaders and they met in the churches of Poland to plan their strategy for such remarkable change. Is not this the work of the Holy Spirit?

In East Germany it was in the churches of Leipzig that the masses first gathered night after night. In Nikolai Church, in downtown Leipzig, peace activists met for months under the direction of the pastor, Christian Fuhrer. The masses grew so large that they spilled out into the streets of the city. Their numbers became so great that openings appeared in the Berlin Wall. In Bucharest, it was the Protestant pastor Laszlo Toekes who sparked the revolution that toppled President Nicolae Ceausescu. It is in the pulpits of the churches of South Africa that the struggle against apartheid was finally successful. John W. DeGruchy, professor of Christian studies at the University of Cape Town said,

> *The church is well placed to be a major part in the building of a new South Africa. It reaches into every village, suburb, and city. It spans cultural and ethnic groups, it speaks the language of the people.*
> — *Christian Century,* Nov. 22, 1989

That sounds to me like an accurate description of the Holy Spirit's activity on the day of Pentecost — spanning race and culture and speaking the language of the people. But, who of us would have ever thought we would live to see a peace treaty between Israel and Palestine, as well as Israel and Jordan? Is not this the work of the Holy Spirit?

Testing The Spirit

Here is a good example that comes to us from the history of the church. In the second century, the church faced such a challenge when Montanus organized an apocalyptic movement. Montanus believed in the speedy outpouring of the Holy Spirit on the church. He believed that he had received direct messages from the Spirit, that the age of the Spirit as foretold in the Gospel of John had returned, and that the second coming of Christ was at hand. Closely associated with him were two women, Prisca and Maximilla. The group practiced ecstatic oracular utterances which they believed to be the evidence of the Holy Spirit. They called themselves "the pneumatics" or the "spiritual church" in contrast to the carnal, lenient and secularized church. The movement was widespread and even Tertullian, the African Church Father, supported the movement. The church was forced to make a decision about this pneumatic movement and at the Asiatic Synod in 200 A.D., Montanism was condemned by the church. Glossolalia, prophecy, and millennarianism of the Montanists has reappeared again and again in widely differing forms. The Christian community cannot escape the challenge of continuing to make such decisions regarding the discerning of the Spirit.

The apostle Paul was one who rejoiced in the Spirit and in the charisma, who gave expression to both the apocalyptic and the enthusiastic, but who also recognized the demonic. James Dunn points out how Paul's gift of discernment provides us with the clearest biblical guidance on how to cope with the darker side of the non-rational and ecstatic (*Expository Times,* Oct. 1982). In our struggle to understand the Spirit's activity in our world and what criteria to use for testing and evaluating, the apostle's method is still a valuable guide. In reviewing the apostle Paul's criteria for discernment and judgment there appear to be four particular tests in deciding if an action or a movement is of the Holy Spirit.

The Test Of Recognized Revelation

First, there is what James Dunn has called the test of recognized revelation. The apostle Paul writes in 1 Corinthians 12:1-4:

> *Now concerning spiritual gifts, brethren, I do not want*
> *you to be uninformed. You know that when you were*
> *heathen, you were led astray to dumb idols . . . . There-*
> *fore I want you to understand that no one speaking by*
> *the Spirit of God ever says "Jesus be cursed!" and no*
> *one can say "Jesus is Lord" except by the Holy Spirit.*

Here is a question regarding spiritual phenomena manifested in the Corinthian church. This was not merely misunderstanding, but real controversy so typical of the Corinthian congregation. Paul warns them against impulses, both individual and collective, in their congregational experiences. Some members are convinced that they were a church guided by the Holy Spirit and that the emotional outbursts occurring in the church were Spirit-inspired. Paul reminds them that their former pagan life had strong emotional outbursts as well, and at that time they were worshipping lifeless idols. He points out that this is not unlike their present situation. William Orr declares that:

> *The turbulent nature of human emotions, especially when*
> *connected with excited religious experiences, may lead to*
> *ideas and actions that are in conflict with the received*
> *traditions and to excessive reliance upon communal feel-*
> *ings. So expressions of the common life that are attributed*
> *to the Spirit must be examined to see whether they may*
> *not be the product of the old, common, human drives*
> *and emotions.*

So Paul is faced with the responsibility of providing the Corinthians with guidelines that will keep them from being carried away by human impulses. As an illustration Paul stresses two extreme exclamations. No one under the guidance of the Holy Spirit will say, "Jesus be damned." Also it is impossible to affirm that "Jesus is Lord," without the power of the

Holy Spirit. The lordship of Jesus is a standard by which to distinguish human impulse and validation by the Holy Spirit.

This affirmation, "Jesus is Lord," was one of the earliest creedal statements of the church. It is the Holy Spirit that guides people to make this affirmation. The Holy Spirit, the apostle is saying, would not cause people to utter the reverse. In Paul's mind this affirmation forms the core of the church's distinctive message. This is the irreducible revelatory data which is at the heart and soul of the new faith. Anything that went against this central affirmation of this new faith was judged to be false prophecy and certainly not the work of the Holy Spirit.

Since we have no other access to the Christ event in human life, except through the New Testament, that means recognizing what James Dunn calls the "normativeness of the New Testament." Therefore, the New Testament is not only presenting what Christianity was, but what Christianity is to be. R. L. Wilken in his book, *The Myth of Christian Beginnings,* points out that Christianity is more than historical process. It is not simply a product of changing cultural contexts or of conflicting social pressures. This is very important for the American church in its temptations toward civil religion and its accommodation with culture. We have a definition of Christianity given to us. We have a norm in which to evaluate what propounds to be a prophetic word for today.

The Test Of Love

Second, we have the test of love. Paul is making a clear case for love in 1 Corinthians 13:4-7:

Love is patient and kind; love is not jealous or boastful; it is not arrogant or rude. Love does not insist on its own way; it is not irritable or resentful; it does not rejoice at wrong, but rejoices in the right. Love bears all things, believes all things, hopes all things, endures all things.

These words were directed to the overzealous charismatics in the Corinthian church who were inspired with their own contribution and importance. He does not doubt or question their devotion, commitment or insight. Simply put, if their accomplishments and achievements do not reflect the character of Christ-like love, then such experiences are a waste of time without value. *If these accomplishments and gifts of the Spirit are loveless, then they are useless.* We need to ask the question: Can truth ever be separated from love? The apostle's answer would be an emphatic, "No!"

Jesus said:

> *By this all men will know that you are my disciples, if*
> *you have love for one another.* — John 13:35

This is the distinguishing mark of Christ's followers. The love that is now characteristic of the Christian community results from Christ's great love for them. Jesus set the example. He calls his disciples to follow his leadings. No actions of the Christian community should ever be separated from the love of Christ. We must always be willing to ask ourselves, "What does the love of Christ demand of me in this situation at this time?" Is it fair to say whatever violates love as expressed in 1 Corinthians 13 is not of the Holy Spirit?

Paul is deeply concerned about the impulses in the Corinthian congregation. These church members were convinced that they were "spirit-led." Their spirituality convinced them they were special, somewhat elitist. They became the antithesis of community. They were divisive, tearing community apart. Their spirituality worked against the Spirit which seeks to build community. They were judgmental bordering on being antinomian, a special spirit-filled people who were above the law. Paul reminds them that the Spirit creates community and love holds community together. Love holds all relationships together. Paul goes on in 1 Corinthians 13 to spell out in very definite terms the substance and nature of this love.

The Test of Community

This leads us to the *third test,* the test of community. This is the test that the apostle constantly applies throughout

1 Corinthians 14. In this chapter Paul defines what he calls the higher and lower gifts. Simply put, he asks: Does it edify the church (community)? Here Paul accuses the Corinthians of majoring in minors, taking a gift of lesser importance, because it does not strengthen the body of Christ, and making it the primary experience of the Christian faith. In this chapter Paul elevates the gift of prophecy above the gift of speaking in tongues. As I have discussed earlier, when judging the gifts of the Spirit Paul asks: Do these gifts benefit and build up community? In 1 Corinthians 14, Paul is showing the relatively unprofitable character of glossolalia in comparison with prophecy. Both are gifts of inspired utterance, but only prophecy engages the total person.

> *For the one who speaks in a tongue speaks not to men but to God; for no one understands him, but he utters mysteries in the Spirit. On the other hand, he who prophesies speaks to men for their upbuilding and encouragement and consolation. He who speaks in a tongue edifies himself, he who prophesies edifies the church.*

The apostle goes on to say that if someone interprets what has been spoken in tongues the church may be edified.

The Test Is Service

Fourth, there is the test of service to God's people. In chapter 14, Paul is saying it is not enough for charisma to be a manifestation of spiritual energy; it must be an act of service to God's people. James Dunn points out that this chapter in 1 Corinthians acknowledges the extent of the spirit's manifestations from the unspectacular act of service to the spectacular ecstatic outburst. Dunn states that the apostle wanted the Corinthians to have a sense of spiritual circumspect that was sensitive enough to recognize when well-meaning people were being misled (*Expository Times*, Oct. 1982, p. 13). The whole point is this: Earliest Christianity took account of the ecstatic and at the same time recognized the need for checks and balances.

> *Thus our own special gifts are enhanced ... by the gifts of others. Without others, our gifts cannot be developed and deepened. With others, our gifts will be checked and limited. Someone has rightly said that God is wanting to do through you what he will not be able to do in all of the future. But how much God can do through you depends on whether your spiritual gifts are employed in the service of others, or self-employed.*
> — Leonard Sweet, *New Life in the Spirit*, p. 77

The Christian community cannot escape the responsibility of evaluating the source and relevance of what is offered today as truth, or whatever claims to be the will of God for the present. Paul's method is still a very valuable tool for us. If it does not pass the tests of recognized revelation, of love, and community benefit, then it flunks the test and is not of the Spirit.

Where is the Spirit of God today? Wherever community is being fashioned, as Sweet reminds us, the Spirit's work in the church, persons, and the world is united. Community is implicit in creation and is brought to life, made manifest, by the power of the Holy Spirit. "The Holy Spirit thus roams the world, not randomly but intentionally, seeking to create communities of learning, reconciliation, compassion, and passion" (Sweet *ibid.* p. 95).

The fact remains that we must discern the meaning and manifestation of God's Spirit in today's world. We are constantly faced with the task of "testing the spirit" to see if the Spirit is of God. One thing is certain: We cannot predict the Spirit's behavior in our midst. The life of the Spirit is so dynamic that the Spirit cannot be preserved in our theological formulas or in our ecclesiastical institutions. The Spirit breaks through all of our formulas and notions about the Spirit.

The dynamics of the Spirit cannot be contained or defined. The Spirit is ever being revealed in the most unexpected ways. There were people and nations who thought they could control and define the Spirit's activity, but life in the Holy Spirit is like a mighty, rushing river, the current so strong no banks can contain it.

Two biblical symbols for the Holy Spirit are wind and fire. These two symbols suggest a fierce ferociousness and tremendous power, but above all they are unpredictable. So is life in the Spirit.

For Further Reflection And Study

1. Where is the Holy Spirit in the world today? What should we be looking for? What are the characteristics of the Holy Spirit that we should be looking for?

2. In what ways does God's activity surprise us?

3. Discuss how God chooses the "least" and the "lowest."

4. What role do you think the Holy Spirit has played in the reform, freedom and liberation movements of the last part of this century?

5. How can we test the spirit to see if it is of God?

6. Comment on the statement that "the Holy Spirit breaks through all of our formulas and notions we have about the Spirit. The dynamics of the Spirit cannot be controlled."

7. How do the biblical symbols of the Holy Spirit (the wind and the fire) relate to the unexpected movement of the Holy Spirit?

8. Where do you think the Holy Spirit is leading our world?

Bibliography

Barth, Karl. *The Holy Ghost and the Christian Life,* Frederick Muller, 1938.

Berkhof, Hendrikus. *The Doctrine of the Holy Spirit,* John Knox Press, 1964.

Brueggemann, Walter. *Hopeful Imagination,* Fortress Press, 1986.

Dunn, James D.G. *Baptism in the Holy Spirit,* Westminster, 1970; *Jesus and the Spirit,* SCM, 1957; *Unity and Diversity in the New Testament,* SCM, 1990.

Forbes, James. *The Holy Spirit and Preaching,* Abingdon, 1989.

Guthrie, Shirley C., Jr. *Christian Doctrine,* John Knox Press, 1968.

Kinghorn, Kenneth C. *Fresh Wind of the Spirit,* Abingdon, 1975.

McFague, Sally. *Metaphorical Theology,* Fortress, 1988.

McKim, Donald. *Theological Turning Points,* John Knox Press, 1988.

Migliore, Daniel L. *Faith Seeking Understanding,* Eerdmans, 1991.

Mills, Watson E. *The Holy Spirit — A Bibliography,* Hendrickson, 1988.

Moltmann, Jurgen. *Creating A Just Future,* Trinity Press, 1989.

Morris, Colin. *The Word and the Words,* Abingdon, 1975.

Phillips, J. B. *The Young Church in Action,* McMillan, 1955.

Rahner, Karl. *The Spirit in the Church,* Seabury, 1979.

Schatzmann, Siegfried. *A Pauline Theology of Chrismata,* Henderickson, 1989.

Stewart, James. *The Wind of the Spirit,* Abingdon, 1968.

Sweet, Leonard I. *New Life in the Spirit,* Westminster, 1982; *The Lion's Pride,* Abingdon, 1987.